101

QUESTIONS

Your pastor hopes you never ask!

DON PAULK
and
EARL PAULK

Printed in the United States of America
ISBN 0-917595-36-X

FOREWORD

by Patricia R. Harwell, RN, MN

Where does a Christian go to find answers to the real questions that thoughtful and often hurting people ask in today's world? To what resources can a Christian address himself or herself with confidence that spiritual truths will be upheld even as practical insight is imparted? This book is a compilation of questions posed and answers given in Wednesday evening services at Chapel Hill Harvester Church in Decatur, Georgia over the past several years.

This is a book which doesn't rely on "pat" answers. Because it comes from the hearts of real people in real life situations, it covers a broad spectrum of human experiences. Difficult topics such as drug abuse, government systems, dysfunctional families, sexuality, abortion and poverty are not avoided.

Some will find this book contains new insight and information. Others will experience this book as an affirming word to ideas and insights already held. Still others will find the answers given to be somewhat unsettling and will feel prompted to greater personal research and study on God's answers for human dilemmas.

In any case, I recommend this book to you as a thoughtful, thought provoking book. Use it as a resource, a study guide and/or a challenge to further growth and comprehension of God's work and presence in the world today.

Patricia R. Harwell

RN, MN is a Marriage and Family Therapist licensed by the state of Georgia. Pat holds a Master's Degree in Psychiatric Nursing earned in 1968 from Emory University. Mrs. Harwell is certified as a Clinical Member and an Approved Supervisor of the American Association of Marriage and Family Therapy and was a member of the Georgia Marriage and Family Counseling Licensing Board from 1978-1980. Since 1980, Mrs. Harwell has been in full-time private practice of individual, marriage and family therapy in the Atlanta area. Mrs. Harwell and her husband, Julian, serve as members and deacons at Chapel Hill Harvester Church.

CONTENTS

PROLOGUE

A pastor sits across the desk from a parishioner who has come for counseling. Running through the pastor's mind is the question, "What am I going to be asked?" There are some areas he really prefers not to talk about. These are the tough questions, the controversial questions. They are the questions he fears being asked. If at all possible, most pastors will avoid having to address these questions. Either they don't know the answers, or they fear the controversy that may be stirred by them.

But what about the brave pastor who is willing to answer these questions? And not only willing to answer them, but to do so publicly. Publicly? Yes, and before hundreds of parishioners plus a television audience. Now, anyone who will attempt this must either know what he is talking about or just be crazy!

Well, here are some of those questions. Over 100 of them, as a matter of fact. You read them and their answers, and you be the judge. After all, an answer is only correct if it solves the problem and does so within scriptural guidelines.

I have been in the ministry now for thirty years . . . all those years in one church. I have heard all these questions asked. And during all these years, I have worked alongside my older brother. He is that brave/foolish/wise pastor who dares answer the hard questions.

For several years on Wednesday nights, these and many hundreds of other questions have been asked. The questions are written down by anyone in the congregation who wishes to ask one. That's my job, asking the questions. Asking is the easy part! But, I admit, I look for the hardest ones. I look for the ones that represent a cross section of whatever most people are asking themselves.

My beloved brother gets to answer the questions. That is the difficult part! But, he has forty-five years of experience in the ministry. He has seen and heard every situation you can imagine. He has had to deal with more than theoretical questions—he has had to find answers for the real problems. There are people who want to know more than where Cain got his wife. They need to know how to deal with a spouse who sexually abuses their kids.

We simply call it "Real Talk". That is literally what it is. You get to ask the question that you always wanted to ask a preacher, but were afraid to ask. Or couldn't find a preacher willing to answer. And when you don't have to sign your name, you can really be candid . . . lower the boom . . . no holds barred. If you want to know . . . ask it!

Thousands of questions have been asked and answered in the past few years. I have kept all of them on file. Now I have gone through them and selected the most asked and most difficult questions. They will interest you. But more importantly, the answers may help you with your own difficult questions of life.

I have discovered that many people have the same problems and ask the same questions. So, it just might be that the elusive answer you have been seeking will turn up right here. If so, then our purpose has been accomplished. Questions anyone? It's time for "Real Talk" . . .

ONE

So, I'm A Christian. What Now?

D o you have questions concerning a call to the ministry or vows made to God? How about dance as a form of worship? Are you concerned about your vocation and how it effects you spiritually? And what is "blasphemy against the Holy Ghost"? Have you ever wondered about telling your pastor something extremely confidential? How do I treat people of other religious convictions? What about "discernment" and "deliverance" in the church? Here are those questions and some answers that may clarify your own questions or perhaps cause you to think . . .

Question:

I have heard you tell how you were supernaturally called into the ministry. I feel I have a call upon my life but I have never experienced anything like you described. Is it possible God can call a person to the ministry in other ways than your own experience?

Answer:

God used various methods to call people in the Bible. John the Baptist leaped in his mother's womb before he was born, whereas Jesus passed Andrew and simply said, "Follow Me, and I will make you a fisher of men." One calling was just as valid as the other. There are a couple of things that are important. First of all, the person has to be convinced that there has been a call upon his life. Secondly, and most importantly, one cannot deny the need for anointing for effective ministry. The results of a ministry are an indication as to the validity of the call. If God calls a person, and that person yields his life, there will be results in his ministry. If a person just enters the ministry out of the conviction that it is just another good vocation and way to make a living, at best the results will be minimal.

Question:

Making vows to God are very serious commitments. If I broke a vow I made to God, how would He punish me?

Answer:

In the first place, a vow to God should not be made lightly. Before a person makes such a vow, he should consider it very seriously and ask the question, "Is this something that I can live with forever?" Once a vow is made, God does indeed take it seriously. However, if we break the vow, God takes no great pleasure in our "punishment." The Scripture says God takes no pleasure in the death of a sinner. However, we should learn valuable lessons from our mistakes. God does indeed chasten us in our mistakes, because He loves us. "Whom the Lord loves, He chastens." But even as a loving parent corrects a child, it is to bring that child to a greater understanding or reach a greater potential or to warn him or her against those things that will destroy him or her. Don't look at God's chastenings as punishment. Consider them as "love licks" to help us find a better way in life.

Question:

We have liturgical dancing here in our church. Many of the movements are the same physical movements I see in "secular" dancing. Please explain the difference in dancing for personal pleasure and dancing unto the Lord. Is it possible that with the appropriate partner (husband/wife) recreational dancing could take on spiritual significance if the motive is to "re-create" the soul of man?

Answer:

Obviously the physical body is used in both liturgical and secular dances. The difference lies in the motive and intentions of the dancer. While a secular dance may draw attention to the creation, the spiritual dance should try to draw attention to the Creator. God is the Creator of harmony and rhythm and grace. Satan has stolen these attributes for his own glory. Our goal is to restore them to their rightful and intended purposes. Also, the "eye of the beholder" is significant. One person can view a dance and receive great spiritual blessing, while another may view it through carnal, lustful eyes. God sees how we view a dance with our own spirits. As to a husband and wife dancing for recreational purposes which may take on spiritual significance, I would say that to the pure all things are pure. Physical exercise is healthy. If a couple dances for this purpose, it is no more evil than any other type of aerobic exercise. There is spiritual significance in all positive things we do. Spirituality is not stained glass windows and spiritual-sounding phrases, or moaning and weeping . . . true spirituality is the more abundant life Christ came to give us!

Question:

In the biblical teaching about the "baptism in the Holy Spirit" the Bible refers to "speaking in other tongues." Exactly what does this mean and do you have to do this in order to evidence that you have received this gift?

Answer:

The promise of the Holy Spirit is made to the believer. "Have ye received the Holy Spirit since ye believed?" (Acts 19:2) That question implies that the Holy Spirit is not available to unbelievers. If a person is skeptical of the gift, he cannot receive it. It is a gift that is available to anyone who will receive it by faith. God does not force any of His gifts upon us. It is true that many Christians live beneath the potential God would give them. The purpose of tongues is to communicate with God. In I Corinthians 14:2 we are told that he who prays in an "unknown tongue prayeth unto God." In this fashion, we pray for things we are not even aware of, for the Holy Spirit knows what we need and makes intercession for us. Even as parents often know what is best for children, even so the Holy Spirit knows better than we what the need is.

Speaking with tongues is an evidence of the Holy Spirit. The six times the Acts of the Apostles records the outpouring of the Holy Spirit, it was accompanied by the evidence of tongues with the exception of Paul, who later said of himself that he thanked God that he spoke in tongues "more than ye all." In my opinion you do not have to speak in tongues in order to be a Christian. But to receive the fullness of the gift of the Holy Spirit, the evidence will be speaking in unknown tongues.

Question:
Is it possible for a born again Christian to be possessed by a demon or evil spirit and remain a Christian?

Answer:
I do not believe that a person who has been born again by the Spirit of God and who has taken on the nature of Christ can be possessed by a demon or demonic force or evil spirit. To be "possessed" indicates "to be controlled by." I do believe that Christians can be "attacked" by demonic forces. That is why Paul instructed the Christian to "put on the whole armor of God" in order to withstand the onslaught and wiles of the devil. We wrestle not against flesh and blood but against principalities and pow-

ers. There would be no need for armor if there were no warfare. Greater is He that is within us than he that is within the world. So, the Christian can be attacked, but not possessed.

Question:

I work for Anheuser-Busch company, which is a national brewery. Even though I don't personally handle the products, sometimes I wonder if I am abetting their overall cause. I have to make a living and it is a good job and I pay my tithes. Should I quit my job and find another one?

Answer:

The Bible says to the pure all things are pure. We can use even good things for evil. Money in a bank can be used for gambling. Gasoline can be used to drive a car fast and kill people. The examples are endless. If you are convinced your position does not contribute directly to the destruction of people, then it is just a way to earn a living. The important thing is not to allow your profession to condemn you. Whatsoever is not of faith is sin, we read in the Bible. If you do feel condemnation, you should consider finding another job.

Question:

I know you have been asked this question hundreds of times, but I need the answer. What is "blasphemy," "the sin unto death" or "the unpardonable sin"?

Answer:

Jesus was accused by some around Him of doing

His work by the power of Beelzebub or Satan. He responded that all sin would be forgiven except that sin of blasphemy. Blasphemy is when one reaches the place in his thinking that he cannot distinguish between good and evil. He begins to attribute the works of God to Satan and the works of Satan to God. When this happens, man so closes out the Spirit of God that he cannot recognize what is right or wrong. The rabid dog has hydrophobia, or a fear of water. That which would save his life is perceived as a threat to him, and he runs from or refuses it. Even so, the very thing that would save a man is what the blasphemous man shuns. It is not that God does not want to pardon or forgive the reprobate person. The reprobate person closes himself off from communication with God, and God cannot reach him.

Question:

As a pastor, many things are told to you in confidence, even criminal activities. What responsibilities do you have to safeguard society to divulge dangerous situations to the authorities? Which is more important—to protect the confidentiality of the person or the safety of the public? What legal or ethical guidelines do you use in making these decisions?

Answer:

Confidentiality is essential in ministry. The premise of "confession" is tied implicitly with the forgiveness of sin. If we are indeed to do the work of Christ on the earth, then a part of His work is the "forgiving" of sin. There is indeed a "cleansing" process that happens in a person who "confesses" to a priest or minister. In secular terms it is known as "getting

something off your chest." The fact is, most things
that are "confessed" to a priest or minister are within
the range of events that all of us are involved with
. . . lying, lusting, infidelity, jealousy, anger, hatred,
etc. Even though these are sinful and ugly, they are
not illegal in many cases. Sinful activities cause people to hurt themselves more than anyone else.

However, there are those situations occasionally
when someone will confess to a crime . . . murder,
stealing, robbing, violence, etc. Ministers and other
associated vocations dealing with the public such as
teachers are now mandated by law to provide certain
types of information. Foremost today is child abuse.
When it is either confessed or if there is reason to
believe it exists, until recently ministers had to report
it on threat of imprisonment for failure to do so. Now
the law states that the clergy "may" report suspected
child abuse. Personally, even though the stated
intent of the law is to protect the public, I see some
implications of it as a foreshadowing of further
government intrusion into the work of the church.

For example, a man confesses to being a bigamist 35 years ago. His first wife is now dead and he
and his second wife have had a good stable relationship for 35 years. Now, on his death bed he confesses
to ease a guilty conscience. No one is aware of this
other wife, not even his "wife" of 35 years. Does the
minister report him to the authorities and cause him
to be publicly judged as a bigamist and scorned by
the family and friends he has established for 35
years? The past cannot be changed now. In my
judgment, exposure would serve no good purpose. To
me, his peace should be made with God. He has
obviously lived in some torment for 35 years. Now he
needs to feel the forgiveness of God before he dies.

The point is, every situation should be judged on its own merits. The guidelines are that we report those mandated situations where there is an obvious threat to another person or persons. We also depend on legal advisors as to when we should report information.

Question:

We have many visits from Jehovah's Witnesses, Mormons, etc., to our door to "convert" us. What should be our response to them? Should we try to "convert" them to Christianity?

Answer:

Whoever comes to your door peacefully is your guest and should be treated with Christian courtesy. However, you should tell them up front that you are a Christian, you are content with your convictions, and you have no intentions of changing your beliefs. As to trying to convert them, they would probably not be at your door on their mission if they were not resolved in their own convictions. However, if they should honestly ask for your testimony, I would give them a testimony of the love of God and your belief in the Lord Jesus Christ. Never argue or debate religion with them. It is a waste of time for both of you. I would simply ask them to respect your convictions, and you do likewise to them. Allow them to leave with a positive encounter of Christian hospitality.

Question:

We speak of bringing back the traditional values of the church with the concept of the Cathedral. Could you explain how this compares to main-line churches under strong charismatic influence doing the same thing?

Answer:

Joel said that God would pour out His Spirit upon all flesh . . . which includes those in main-line traditional churches. The only criterion is an open spirit to receive the gift provided to all believers. Perhaps it might be said that we are trying to accomplish the same thing coming from two different directions. Many in main-line traditional churches have never been exposed to the spontaneity of the Spirit. They have had the "form," but the "power" has been lacking. We come from the other perspective. Many in our church were raised in "Pentecost" and are aware of the "moving of the Spirit" and are able to spontaneously "flow." However, their background has been casual, and in some cases, unorthodox. They lack the rich tradition and heritage of the orthodox church. Much theological error has been espoused in dispensational, Pentecostal churches. The balance of orthodox or scriptural teachings is then important for their spiritual maturity.

In my opinion, there needs to be a revival throughout the entire body of Christ. We need to embrace and to espouse sound theological doctrine that can be scripturally validated. There needs to be great emphasis placed on the role of the Holy Spirit not only in the life of the believer, but also in the administration of the Church. For that reason, we call our Cathedral the Cathedral of the Holy Spirit.

Question:

We hear a lot about discernment and how important it is. Common sense tells you some things about situations. You don't have to have a special gift to figure them out. Explain the difference in intuition, good judgment, common

sense and discernment.

Answer:

Discernment is a spiritual gift. There are many similarities with the other qualities. Discernment often embodies common sense, good judgment, and intuition. These qualities are available to nonspiritual people, and even unbelievers. However, discernment has a quality the others lack. For that reason, these people have to depend upon the obvious. The obvious can often be deceptive. A person who has the gift of discernment can see beyond the obvious and detect deeper spiritual ramifications of a situation. The purpose of discernment is for the protection of the church. It is never for the purpose of "fortune-telling" or "reading people's minds" and that sort of thing.

Question:

A friend of mine recently attended a "deliverance" service where they cast out demons by regurgitating in a trash can. Is this a valid form of exorcism?

Answer:

This form of deliverance has never been a part of my ministry. I can find no scriptural basis for it in the Bible. However, to categorically deny that it can be valid is not my purpose. The proof of ministry is in its results and effectiveness. Often God uses methods that transcend our human comprehension. We are emotional creatures. If a person feels that by "regurgitating" a spirit up, he has relieved himself of that spirit, then if later that spirit does not trouble him, who is to judge that such an experience didn't work? The error in any method is when we begin to believe that God always uses the same method every time, and even condemn others who don't use that same technique.

Question:

I have been in services where many people were "slain in the spirit," many of them falling in a "wave" across the congregation. What is your interpretation of this?

Answer:

There is a reference in the Bible where the "cloud" of God was so great in the House of God that the people were effected by this overwhelming presence of God. However, most accounts of people being "slain" involve people in rebellion. Saul of Tarsus was on his way to persecute the Christians when he was struck down. Of course, the ultimate slaying was literal when Ananias and Sapphira lied to the Holy Spirit and were fatally slain! My experience is that God wants our willing obedience. If we say we will not do something, in all likelihood, that is what God will require of us. He wants our total commitment. If a person vows he will not be "slain" or fall out, God may prove him wrong! God has the right to do anything He chooses. Don't overlook the power of suggestion. It is not unusual for crowds to respond similarly when everyone is reacting in a certain way. No one wants to feel different or isolated, even in spiritual things. But I don't see it as a regular, ongoing method of ministry within the church.

TWO

It's Not My Fault, Is It?

My marriage is falling apart . . . what do I do? I am single. What about my sexual urges? Is there life after divorce? What do I do with my jealous spouse? My husband has a "friend." How should I respond to her? What about interracial marriages? How do blacks and whites get along together? These are the areas discussed in this chapter. Compare your answer with these . . .

Question:

I have a Christian brother. We don't agree on many things. As a matter of fact, we disagree on more things than we agree. I love him very much and have prayed and fasted on how to handle the strain of the relationship. Do I give up or hold on to a friendship that causes such pain?

Answer:

It could be that God is using you vicariously in the life of your brother. The virtue of forgiveness can be greatly demonstrated here. We are to forgive our brother who mistreats or wrongs us "seventy times seven" . . . each day, or better understood, as many times as necessary. I don't suggest giving up a relationship because of pain, although God may lead you to lovingly detach from that person for a while so that the Holy Spirit can get his or her attention. A loving mother is pained by an erring son but it may well be her patience and her prayers that may bring that son to God or to a change of his ways. A true friend loves at all times . . . even in times of pain.

Question:

Are interracial or intercultural marriages sinful?

Answer:

Interracial or intercultural marriages are not sinful. Even though we bring our racial and cultural heritages into marriage, we must remember that when people marry, they become "one" and give up their "rights" as individuals. We no longer belong to ourselves. Often the scripture that says we should not be "unequally yoked together" is quoted to support the notion that God does not approve of interracial marriages. What the scripture is teaching here is that believers should not be yoked or married to unbelievers. In the Bible, God directed that nationalities marry within their own nation because He was doing a special work in that nation. Today, God is doing a special work within His Church and He desires it to remain strong. The divisiveness that often occurs within marriages where one is an unbeliever often destroys those homes. Even though some within our society try to interpret the scripture to read that interracial marriage is sinful, there is no scriptural basis to support this opinion.

Any interracial couple that marries should be aware, however, that there will be many obstacles to overcome in such a marriage. The couple must be prepared to bear the stigma that society often attaches to these unions. They must also consider the far-reaching effects that it may bring to their own children. Children of mixed racial backgrounds are often isolated by both races. Even as we give up our personal rights to our companions when we marry, a couple gives up some of their rights to their offspring when they become parents. The wise couple considers every aspect of a relationship before they decide to marry. Above all, they need the wisdom of God to make their union a successful marriage.

Question:

My husband and I were separated for nine months. I moved out and left him. He began seeing someone else. Then we reconciled and

are getting along wonderfully. Now we find out the woman he was seeing during that time is five months pregnant. What do we do now?

Answer:

There are consequences to sin even for Christians. Obviously, the marriage had not been dissolved, and the man was not free to pursue another intimate relationship. Even though his behavior was wrong, it is not an unpardonable sin. Hopefully, this wife has forgiven her husband and is ready to do her part to solve the problem. He does bear the responsibility of the child that was conceived. Now he should also bear the responsibilities and consequences of that relationship that produced this child. As a part of the rebuilding of the relationship with this wife, they together must solve this problem. He does have a responsibility to the woman in all matters relating to the child. He should not do anything in secret to meet these responsibilities. He should be totally open with this wife about how he is solving the problem while making the mother of the expected child aware that his wife is aware of all decisions concerning his meeting his responsibilities to his child. It can serve to deepen the relationship between him and his wife while establishing the end of the intimate relationship with the other woman. The care and raising of that child is an ongoing responsibility. A father's responsibility doesn't end with a child's birth, it is just the beginning.

Question:

I am a twelve-year-old girl and I want to date older boys. Is this wrong? What age do you think young people should start dating?

Answer:

It is not uncommon for twelve-year-old girls to want to date older boys. Girls mature physically and emotionally earlier than boys, and they are more comfortable with older boys. All "dating" at this age should be in group settings. I don't think it is appropriate to "single date" at this age. Even though the degree of maturity varies with each individual and their own training, etc., I think a girl should be about 16 before she begins "single dating." Even then, it should be casual dating. In my judgment, young people today make mistakes to settle into "going steady" too soon. There is plenty of time later for serious relationships. Get to know the personalities and characteristics of various people to see what you really want in a person. Serious dating that could lead to marriage should not take place with a girl before her late teens. As a matter of fact, people are getting married later in life these days. I think that is a healthy trend. Maturity always proves to be an asset to a marriage.

Question:

I have a friend who is a Christian who began dating an atheist. Now she suddenly has begun to question the existence of God. Has she blasphemed God? What responsibility or judgment will he have for fostering her disbelief?

Answer:

This a classic example of the reason God said not to be "unequally yoked together." She opened herself to this possibility when she knowingly entered the relationship. In my judgment, she hasn't changed her beliefs about God as much as she is trying to please her boyfriend by appearing to have accepted his beliefs. Even though she hasn't blasphemed, if she continues on this path, she could well become reprobate, closing out God's ability to deal with and speak to her. As for his responsibility, God said that it is better that a millstone be put about your neck and be cast into the sea than to offend a little one. This verse refers to people who destroy one's faith in Jesus Christ. Yes, he will bear that responsibility. Often young people claim to be "atheists" because it supposedly makes them sophisticated and intellectual. As a friend to both of them, try to reach out to them with love, showing them the goodness of God. The Bible says that it is the goodness of God that brings men to repentance . . . not intellectual prowess!

Question:

I am a single woman. I have a married male friend who wants me to play tennis, have dinner, etc., with him. Is this appropriate?

Answer:

Even though it is not a sin for a single woman to play tennis or have dinner with a married man, there are some inherent dangers to consider. First of all, does the man's wife know and approve of the friendship? Does it detract from his attention to his own wife? Does it limit your ability to seek a relationship with a single man? Also, you must be aware that even casual relationships often mature into deeper relationships. Ask yourself the question, "What is the long range purpose of this relationship? Does it benefit everyone involved?" If a relationship does not serve a positive purpose in everyone's life who is involved, then it has no right to exist. If you have no desire to have this type of friendship with him, then simply be honest and tell him that you do not want to play tennis, have dinner, etc.

Question:

I have been married six years and my wife and I have two young daughters. Now she tells me she no longer loves me and wants out of the marriage. She says she only married me hoping she would grow to love me, but she never did. Should we stay together for the sake of the children knowing she doesn't want to be with me, or should we each take one of the children and split them up, or should we face the truth and get a divorce? What do you suggest?

Answer:

Covenants made before God are not made on the basis of whether love exists or not. The covenant is still valid regardless of falling in or out of love! The primary consideration now is indeed the children. Every effort should be made to conceal any conflict between the two of you from them, especially if they are young children. Perhaps you haven't created an atmosphere for your love to take root and grow. It would be a tragedy not only for the home to be broken, but it also compounds the tragedy to break up the children. Every effort should be made not only to reconcile, but also to create a love relationship. Love indeed can be cultivated if there was once a seed of attraction. Try to return to what originally drew you together. Finally, I would suggest you seek good Christian counseling.

Question:
If you have been divorced for any reason other than fornication, will God forgive you and approve another marriage?

Answer:
It is a sin to marry outside of God's provisions and will, but it is not an unforgivable sin. God will forgive this sin. It is necessary to ask God's forgiveness. Attempting to undo mistakes in our lives is impossible. For example, some people have asked whether they should divorce their second spouses and remarry their first spouses. Two wrongs do not equal one right! The important factor in finding God's will is to establish the marriage you are in now on the firm foundation of Jesus Christ.

Question:
I am soon to be married to a 39-year-old woman. We want to have children but are concerned about complications that may come with a pregnancy at this age. What do you think?

Answer:
If your mutual agreement and desire is to have a child in your marriage, I think you should commit it to the will of God and move toward realizing your dream. Your mental attitude is very important in this decision. You should enter into your pregnancy with a positive attitude, expecting all to be well. I would think that if you are in good health and are under good medical care, there should be no problem. I restate that I think your positive mental attitude is very important.

Question:
I have been married to a very possessive man for twenty-seven years. I have to account for every minute of my time, such as where I go, and my phone calls are censored and monitored. I have given him no cause to be jealous—either before or during our marriage. I am just about ready to bail out of a very unhappy situation. What should I do?

Answer:
The Bible says that jealousy is crueler than the grave. It can result in great misery for both parties. Jealous people are miserable people. If indeed you have done nothing to precipitate his jealousy, then he has a serious problem. He obviously is controlled by a spirit of jealousy. If he is a Christian, he needs deliverance from this spirit. If he is not a Christian and is not open to spiritual guidance and help, then perhaps he might submit to some type of professional counseling. I assume you have calmly confronted him with your feelings and have reassured him he has no need to be jealous. The last resort is to "bail out" of the situation. If he becomes physically abusive, that presents another problem. Civil laws protect women from violence at the hands of their husbands. Never hesitate to seek the help and protection of authorities if this violation should occur.

Question:
I have been divorced for several years now. My ex-husband still wants to maintain a good relationship with me. That is alright. But how far should it go? When we were married, we never had any sexual problems. Our problems

were in other areas, but they were serious enough to end the marriage. It is as if he is wanting to continue the "good" part of our relationship, which was physical. I admit, I still enjoy a sexual relationship but not enough to try to live with him as husband and wife. The pain is still there. What should I do?

Answer:

No physical relationship, no matter how satisfying it may be, is enough to hold a relationship together. When the physical is gone, he will be gone also. If you did not have enough other things to maintain the marriage, it is inappropriate to allow sex to keep you tied to him emotionally. If that relationship is truly over, end all aspects of it and move on to some relationship in which you may find complete fulfillment. As it is, he is preventing you from developing other potentially permanent relationships. As long as you will allow it, he will take advantage of you. But when the sex is gone, he will be gone also.

Question:

For two years my wife and I have encountered marital problems, mostly stemming from the fact we have no children. I have a 15-year-old from a previous marriage, which my wife resents. She says she wants to be the mother of her own children. She heard that there were Mexican children available for adoption. She insisted we adopt them to the point of threatening to divorce me and adopt them as a single parent if I didn't agree to her plans. In our present financial situation, and because of the friction in our marriage, I don't think adoption would be wise at this time. I went through one painful divorce. I don't want us to suffer through that. I understand her need to mother children. Are there other alternatives?

Answer:

There is a built-in need in women to have their own children. It is also true that there is often resentment of children from previous marriages, especially if she has no children of her own to take up her devotion. I would strongly suggest good counseling about this situation. If adoptions are made as a result of threats, that could create problems later. Threatening to divorce and adopt as a single parent suggests a quality of desperation or obsession about having a child. Counseling could help bring this need into a place of balance in her life. Also, I would carefully investigate the legality of Mexican adoptions. I have heard of people who were disappointed by promises of children like this in which the person would pay certain fees, but the children were never secured. I would assure her that you want her to be a mother, but only under the proper circumstances.

Question:

My spouse contends that healthy marriages often include other relationships or friends. I believe that I should be able to provide everything he needs . . . companionship, friendship, counsel, recreation. There should be no occasion for any other relationship in his life other than casual friendship. Am I wrong?

Answer:

Other appropriate relationships should not be

viewed as threats to a good marriage. If a marriage is secure, other relationships will never threaten it. The question then becomes what is an appropriate relationship outside of marriage. Actually, it is rare that one person can meet every need that another person has. Even though we assume that our spouse can meet most of our needs better, there may still remain areas in which other friends meet specific needs. For example, if a husband is an avid sportsman, would the wife be willing to stand on a freezing deer stand all day, camp out in the wilderness, wade cold streams, skin dead animals and other things a hunter may do? Or, can a husband spend an entire day at the shopping mall looking at hundreds of items, comparing their value, price, etc.? The fact is, we often do need other kinds of relationships to complete our lives. Also, consider your motives for wanting your spouse all to yourself. Is it really a sign of confidence in your ability to meet all his needs, or is it a sign of insecurity that he may indeed find someone else who can meet his needs better than you? Often we stifle relationships by being together too much! It is better to have quality time in which we fully enjoy being together rather than quantity time when you begin to get on each other's nerves.

Question:

I was recently devastated by a relationship that went sour and now I feel so alone. As I think of developing new relationships, my mind always goes back to this man who betrayed my trust and love. How do I get over this devastating experience and move on to other relationships?

Answer:

You must realize first that you should not judge all men by the failures of one man. Just because you cannot trust that man does not mean no men exist whom you can trust. The best way to overcome the pain of a failed relationship is to establish a meaningful and fulfilling relationship with someone else. Obviously, you will be cautious because of your past experiences. But let the past be a learning experience. Now you should know what characteristics to look for in a man. We all make mistakes in relationships. Don't repeat the same mistakes. But to withdraw and isolate yourself because of a sour relationship will not solve problems. Such isolation only brings more loneliness. There is always someone, somewhere, who can help take away the pain and loneliness if we are receptive to new relationships.

Question:

I understand the great responsibility of a mother being home with her children, especially when they are small. But with today's cost of living, my family cannot make it financially without both me and my husband working. Is this wrong for me to work even though I wish I could be at home with my children?

Answer:

The influence of the mother is so important in a child's life, especially in the lives of very small children. Children always need their parents, but some phases of life are more critical than others. The mother's closeness is important the first days of a child's life. However, in today's economy, sometimes we do not have options in order to make ends meet.

Look closely at your budget to make sure that every effort has been made to live within the available funds. If you are convinced there are no alternatives, then don't feel guilty about subsidizing the family income. If your working is necessary, every effort should be made to minimize its effect on the children. Spend as much quality time with them as possible. The input and participation of the father is equally important. Some women are happier with careers. If this working does not jeopardize the welfare of the family, then it is not a sin. But the first responsibility of a parent, and especially of a mother is her children, and especially small children or infants.

Question:

I was married for a number of years before I divorced. I have never had any sexual relationship with any man other than the man I married. Now I have developed a romantic relationship with a man. Because a physical relationship was so natural to me in my years of married life, I find it difficult to draw lines as to what is acceptable intimacy as a single Christian. Help me draw the right guidelines.

Answer:

Sexual desires are not evil, they are normal. However, you must ask yourself what you want to do with your life now. Will you be content to settle for just a sexual outlet as a substitute for a complete relationship? You should do everything possible to place this relationship on a secure foundation. Sex alone will not last. If the new man in your life is interested in a permanent relationship, he will want to establish it on the right foundation as well. There

are three guidelines I would recommend to you. 1.
What kind of quality life and relationship do I want?
2. Do I want to live in a posture of guilt for inappropriate sexual actions? 3. Is God preparing a relationship for me that I may jeopardize if I don't respond
with proper restraints at the appropriate time?

Question:
Some churches infer that the black race is the result of a plague or curse God placed upon them. Is this true?

Answer:
It is totally inaccurate to suggest that race has
anything to do with a curse or a plague. Any biblical
reference to the dissemination of races or languages
would have to refer to the Tower of Babel where people attempted to build a tower to the heavens in order
to become god-like. At that point, God confused their
language and scattered them geographically. No
mention is made that any changes in color occurred.
The point of the "curse" here was not racial, but
because mankind sought to become "like God." This
was the same sin Adam and Eve had committed, trying to become "like God" or gods unto themselves.
Moses married an Ethiopian black woman, and
Miriam, Moses' sister, was stricken with leprosy after
she and her brother Aaron complained about it.
There is no biblical reason for the variations of skin
color. We can assume it came about by climate differences or perhaps God chose to use variety in His
human creation. Even as He created various hues of
flowers and there are color differences in the animal
kingdom, it could be that God wanted variety in
mankind. No curse is associated with skin color

according to Scripture.

Question:
Why are more crimes committed by blacks than whites in this country?

Answer:
Crime has nothing to do with skin color. It has to do with the environments that create a climate for crime, the lack of education, the lack of vocational skills, and the lack of job opportunities. Crime is synonymous with deprivation and poverty, prejudice and inequity. Black Africans were brought to this country as slaves. Since that time, their struggle has been long, and their plight has made it difficult to achieve their place in society. The result forces many black citizens to lives of crime in order to survive. Lack of education and other opportunities in our society have embittered many blacks, and they have become angry. The fruit of bitterness is often violence. Even though statistics may reflect a higher crime rate per capita among blacks, it only reflects the consequences of the problems I have mentioned, not the fact that skin color suggests a propensity for crime.

Question:
Do you approve of an emphasis upon "black history" in our schools?

Answer:
I approve of history. History is merely an account or record of the events of the past. Obviously, black people in this country have played a significant role. Once an event has passed, we are dependent upon

the "story-tellers"—newspapers, written accounts, documents, legal records, etc., in order to preserve what events actually happened. Many true accounts are recorded, but I realize there are many points of history that have been shaded by "story-tellers" for various reasons. The fact is, many significant blacks in history have been overlooked by these accounts. Martin Luther King, Jr., George Washington Carver and a handful of blacks show up in our history books. Thousands of others also played important roles who are never mentioned. For this reason, "black history" was developed in order to preserve those who were excluded. It is time that history reflects the total picture, not just a partial, racially biased, one-sided picture.

Question:

Why is the black society a strong "matriarchal" culture? Why do so many black men refuse to accept the responsibilities of their families, forcing the women to be the heads of their households?

Answer:

In days of slavery in this country, families were separated more often than not. Children stayed with the mother for obvious reasons . . . they were nursed and cared for by the mother. Black slave men were valuable to their owners as workers, not fathers. Later on, the welfare system created the need for adverse circumstances in order for the home to survive as a unit. Because welfare benefits could be received by a single woman with children, it encouraged the black male to live away from the mother and the children. These are social circumstances that have created and perpetuated a social problem. The need for strong male headship in the black home is as great as that need in any other race. But, people often have to adapt to the social conditions in order to survive.

Question:
Do you approve of civil disobedience in order to attain civil rights?

Answer:
I do not approve of violent means to accomplish anything. Martin Luther King, Jr. learned a valuable lesson from Henry David Thoreau and Mahatma Gandhi, and that was the concept of non-violent resistance. As painful as it can be, non-violence is still the most effective method for achieving a desired end. Passive resistance can be an effective tool, and it is not demeaning nor destructive. I have often been alarmed at some activist's willingness to bomb abortion centers with the very possible risk of killing people on the conviction of saving unborn fetuses. Is not one life as valuable as another, even the life of the teenaged girl who may be in that clinic at the time the bomb explodes? The sanctity of human life and respect for property should extend to all, even to those with whom we disagree. We have a right and an obligation to express our dissent, but never in a violent or destructive manner.

Question:
I am a black woman married to a white man. He always sees issues as black/white. He constantly remarks that certain things happen because of the inherent nature of blacks. Even

though we all have our cultural and ethnic backgrounds as a part of our total personalities, wouldn't it be better to judge issues on individual merit, not merely generalize that our race dictates our responses? I ask this question because I wonder if you would give some advice to people contemplating an interracial marriage. What are the important things we should consider?

Answer:

It is always unfortunate when one race generalizes behavior about another race and infers that certain traits are inherent to that race. While social circumstances may have created similar problems for individuals within a race, that does not mean there are "racial" traits that all possess. There is nothing scriptural that prohibits interracial marriages. However, often differences are created by environmental backgrounds. There are many social problems that an interracial couple will face: acceptance by both races, both families, racially mixed children and a long list of issues to deal with daily. Before a couple enters marriage, I would strongly recommend premarital counseling both with spiritual leaders and with professional marriage counselors to prepare adequately for the marriage. Marriages today have a difficult time surviving, especially interracial ones. They need to begin on a strong foundation.

THREE

What's A Parent To Do?

My teenager is out of control. Is there help? Is spanking the best way to correct our kids? What about this crazy music they listen to . . . should I put my foot down and say "no"? I found out my kid is experimenting with drugs. What do I do? My daughter has started taking birth control pills. What should my response be? What's the truth about child abuse? Grandma still thinks she is in charge. How do I deal with her? My kid sucks her thumb. Should I worry?

There is no more frustrating era than that of raising children today. There are so many pitfalls for parents. Here are some answers to not only the questions you ask but the questions the kids themselves ask us . . .

Question:

I hear my parents use curse words. I hear them on TV, in the movies, and in music. I hear politicians using them. Yet, I am told I shouldn't use them. Is it wrong? Are some curse words worse than others?

Answer:

Out of the mouth, the heart speaks. Certain patterns tell people who we are: the way we dress; the way we behave; the things we say. All of these tell people about our character. People use profanity for various reasons. Some do it to sound tough. Some do it to emphasize their points. Some do it out of habit. Some do it because that is all they have ever heard from their parents and their friends. Some think it adds color to their vocabulary. Some do it to be accepted by their peers. Whatever the reasons, when foul language is excessive, it becomes crude and tasteless. It tells people you have a limited vocabulary and are having to resort to "street" talk in order to communicate. Some words are "slang," while others are profane. Some "slang" terms are derivatives of profane words. For example, "heck" obviously is a contraction of "hell"; "darn" a derivative of "damn"; and even "gee" a form of "Jesus." I would suggest to young people that they become students of their language and learn to use descriptive words that make their conversations bright and entertaining without resorting to obscenities. And yes, some profane words are worse than others. Some words are dirty and nasty and allude to common human functions. Others take the name of God in vain and violate the commandment that says not to "take the name of the

Lord thy God in vain." Coarse language insults not only the one who hears it, but also the one who utters it. It is a form of "air pollution." I would suggest that you keep the "air" clean around you!

Question:

I am a 15-year-old girl. I have no interest in boys, at least in a "romantic" way. I prefer to be around girls. Am I gay?

Answer:

At 15 years of age, you are just beginning to establish your identity. Perhaps your feelings of sexuality haven't totally formed yet. Perhaps you haven't had a particularly good relationship with your father or have come from a broken home where your father has been regarded negatively. It could be that you don't think you are attractive to boys, so you gravitate to "safe" relationships with other girls where you don't base your acceptance upon your looks. At your age, I don't really think you are gay. However, I would suggest good Christian counseling in order to direct your focus toward healthy heterosexual relationships in the future.

Question:

I am 17 years old. My dad usually has a beer when he comes home from work. My parents drink wine with their meals occasionally. I don't recall ever seeing either of them drunk. I would assume they are what you would call "moderate" drinkers. Is it wrong for me to drink and smoke pot in moderation?

Answer:

There are several very important considerations here. First of all, the matter of setting an example for others. Even though the Bible does not teach total abstinence, but moderation, there is a greater issue of setting the proper example before impressionable people, especially children who watch adults and assume that anything we do is alright. One never knows what his own body chemistry or metabolism may be. One person may be able to drink a beer or a glass of wine regularly without becoming addicted, whereas we have learned that some people are "born" alcoholics. That is, they cannot tolerate alcohol in their system without becoming addicted very easily. The father who drinks a beer before his son may not suffer alcoholism himself, but he may start his son on a course of addiction. The greatest cause of fatal accidents among young people is alcohol related. This is tragic!

As for "pot," the information is not in on the long-range effects of habitual drug users. Obviously we know that cocaine, crack, heroin and some of these drugs are ultimately deadly. The evidence is beginning to mount now against the use of marijuana. At one time considered to be harmless and non-addictive, evidence is proving otherwise today. Even though it may not be addictive physiologically, it becomes addictive emotionally. People like the feeling they have when they use it, and they continue to use it. It dulls their senses and renders them very vulnerable. It is also being proven that it affects our children. Is it worth damaging the potential of an unborn child to get "high" now? The fact is, addiction is addiction, whether it be alcohol or drugs. The end result of addiction is the same. It often leads to devastation and destruction, and the greatest sin is the wasted potential of a human life.

Question:

I am a teenager. I am saved, filled with the Holy Spirit and go to church regularly, yet I feel very empty. I don't want to be perceived as a religious nut, "Bible-totin' " praise maniac, but I do want to feel God move in my life. What is wrong with me?

Answer:

We often equate spirituality with emotion. It is true that many people have physical responses when they worship. It is also true that some stand quietly, perhaps with a hand raised or tears trickling down their cheeks who are experiencing the same spirit of worship as the person in the aisle doing the "Pentecostal shuffle." An old saying can be applied here: "What you do speaks so loudly that I can't hear what you are saying." The life of the Christian is a life of example. He is told to be a "light" to the world, not a "noise." Lights make very little noise! When God saves us, we indeed become new creatures in Christ, but He only cleans up our personalities, not completely changes them. If you were a quiet sinner, you will probably be a quiet Christian. If you were a loud sinner, you may well be a loud Christian. God created a variety of personalities. The important thing is that you feel a confidence in your experience with Christ. Your worship should be directed to God to please Him—not to please or excite or impress those about you.

Question:

Is it wrong for boys to wear earrings today? Fashions change. What was not accepted widely a few years ago is now the norm.

Answer:

Often there is "more than meets they eye" in a situation. For example, fashions often give us subtle messages with coded or hidden meanings. In some circles boys wearing earrings in their ears inform people that they are homosexual. The earring is a coded message to give that information. Fashions can also uncover rebellious spirits. How often do we see teens dressing in a bizarre way in order to make a statement of independence from their parents. Also, there is a trend to erase clothing lines of identification between male and female. Some fashion trend setters would move to what they call "unisex," that is, fashions preventing you from telling the difference between the sexes. God did not create unisex— He created male and female. But to say it is a sin for a boy to wear an earring would be going too far. It depends on his motive and what he is attempting to convey. It could have its advantages. Rather than the teenaged son asking to borrow the car Saturday night, he could ask mom if he could borrow her earrings!

Question:

How do parents deal with a teenager who is totally out of control and in rebellion against all authority?

Answer:

By the time a child reaches the teen years if he is

out of control and in rebellion against authority, it is an indication that the problem began many years earlier. We cannot wait until a child reaches his teens to begin molding and training him. Discipline should begin while he is a very small child. You can't undo the past, but perhaps you can take a different approach with him that may have some positive effects.

At this stage in life you must deal with teens' minds and their spirits. Physical punishment at the teenage level, especially in the late teens and particularly with girls, will only drive them further from you. The important focus at this stage is to try to develop a relationship with them. First I would appeal to their sense of reason. Point out that they are no longer children, and they wish to be treated as adults. But along with adult privileges come adult responsibilities. Outline those responsibilities—which should include respecting their authorities at home, school, work, etc. Point out that in the real adult world we all have to respect authority, or we end up as criminals, or fired from jobs, or expelled from school. Point out that in the adult world when a rule or law is broken, that there is a penalty to pay. If he breaks the rules you or the school or even a civil law have established, then he must be prepared to pay the consequences.

I would choose those things your teen particularly enjoys and use those activities as areas of correction. Notice I said "correction," not punishment. Punishment says you don't love them. Correction should convey love and concern. If they enjoy talking on the phone with their friends, one thing you might do is limit or ban their use of the telephone for a reasonable period. Always make the "punishment" fit the "crime." That is, mete out correction to the degree of the severity of the infraction. Car privileges if they drive, permission for social activities and these types of things can be used in correction. Never take away church activities as a form of punishment. Never use God to correct. It pictures Him in their minds as a tool of punishment. If there is no response, then you should seek professional help. Perhaps drugs or alcohol abuse may be at the core of the problem. Learn the signs of recognizing these problems, and don't hesitate to get both spiritual and professional help.

Question:

I am eleven years old. If your parents are divorced and you love them both, which one should you live with? I want to live with my dad, but he's never home, and I want to stay with my mom because she loves me like my dad does, and also I won't be staying home alone. What would you do?

Answer:

The real solution to this problem lies in the cause of the problem—the parents. Let me address them first. One of the most tragic problems in our society today is graphically portrayed in this question. In divorce the victims are always the children. They are the innocent bystanders who get killed in the wars between parents who cannot get along. Suffice it to say, most husbands and wives have marital problems to some degree. But how we handle those problems is very important. We should never allow our children to become the battleground or involve them in emotional tugs of war. Even though we may have differences, we should agree on one thing: the best interest of our children who did not ask to be born. If divorce is inevitable, the parents should agree on conditions that best accommodate the children. Children should stay with the parent who is best suited and equipped to provide care. Visitation rights should be fair and should be adhered to religiously. Nothing is more important than spending time with your children when they are looking forward to being with you. Divorce means that they have been disappointed enough by their parents. Don't compound the injury! I would remind the child that parents do make mistakes. Even though they can't get along with each other, that doesn't mean they don't love you. You should show your love to both of them.

Question:

Is the "rod of correction" mentioned in Proverbs 29:15 to be interpreted as literal or symbolic? Spanking seems to be a lazy way to discipline children. This takes away their self-esteem and makes them feel unloved. It seems there are better ways of correcting children. What do you think?

Answer:

Spanking can indeed be the easy way out of disciplining children. It can also be nothing more than a vent for anger toward someone else that is directed toward the child. A child should never be spanked when a parent is angry. There should always be a "cooling off" period to prevent spanking from seeming abusive. As children mature, it is important to deal with their minds and spirits rather than resort to physical correction. When a boy reaches a certain

51

age, he often will bear the physical punishment in exchange for doing whatever he wants to do if he considers the deed worth the price of the pain! Most experts agree that spanking as a form of correction loses its effect at about age ten. But there is also a spiritual truth involved here. The Bible says if we spare the rod, we spoil the child. A permissiveness dominates many parents. Those parents often reap severe behavioral problems in their children as the children grow older. Spankings should always be administered with love. It truly hurts the parent more to discipline than it does the child. You only realize that truth after you become a parent. But spanking children in an appropriate way at the right time under the right circumstances is sometime necessary. It cannot be replaced by any new method that is conceived in our society today.

Question:

I have often heard about the "age of accountability" being twelve years old. That is considered to be the time we become responsible for our sins in the eyes of God. I wonder that with the sophistication and enlightenment of our children today, that age isn't far younger. At what age should we lead our children into a salvation experience with Jesus Christ?

Answer:

There is no way to arbitrarily select an age of accountability that applies to all children. Environment, training, and teaching of children vary greatly. I do believe that children are aware of many things earlier now than when parents were committed to sheltering and protecting their children from the realities of life. As soon as a child can understand right from wrong, realize that doing something wrong is a "sin," and that sin must be forgiven by Jesus Christ, I think they are old enough to receive Christ as their Savior. We should put the message of salvation on a very simple basis so that they can understand. Even young children can understand that they don't always do the right or good thing. They can also understand that Jesus loves "sinners" and forgives them of their sins if He is asked to forgive them. They may not understand fully that they are "sinners" but they can understand that Jesus loves us so much that He died for us to prove His love even though we do make mistakes or are "sinners." And they can understand that because we believe ‛that Jesus died for us because He loved us, we can live as Christians. A child could understand a parent who would risk his life to save theirs. Even so, when they can understand this, they can understand enough to be "saved." I wouldn't specify a specific age for salvation, but it could well be in the single digits of a child's life. Statistics prove that most Christians are saved while they are young, and most of them before they reach twelve years of age.

Question:
Music plays such an important role in our lives and especially in the lives of our children and teens. What secular music is appropriate to be allowed in the home? What music should be totally forbidden to young people?

Answer:
I don't know the names of some of the "heavy metal" bands, but I do know that the lyrics of some

of their songs are not only suggestive, but also outright evil. Even secular groups of people have recognized this and are calling for legislation to control the lyrics dealing with all forms of sexual aberration, violence, murder, incest, death, suicide, abortion, drugs, alcohol and social irresponsibility. Such lyrics foster rebellion against any authority. Indeed, many of the behavior problems of our youth can be traced directly to the influence of music in their lives. This influence is far greater than we even realize. Music is probably one of the three most important identifications in a young person's life. I do not object to all secular music. Much secular music is enjoyable. Some lyrics are pleasant, and they speak of love and caring relationships. I would suggest parents periodically check what their kids are listening to. Don't monitor in a hostile way. Perhaps a parent just wanders in as teens are listening to music, and the parent asks them to decipher the lyrics. Most of us can't understand what the band is saying. It is almost as if it were sung in code! Ask teens to tell you what they think of the lyrics. Do they think the message benefits them? At some point it may be necessary to calmly but firmly forbid the purchase of recordings by certain heavy metal groups. Hit a happy medium in your attitude. Just because you may not enjoy rock and roll music or jazz doesn't mean it's all wrong. Don't base your decisions for your teens on the basis of your own personal musical taste, but on the quality of the lyrics. But I do think certain driving, cacophony of sounds are demonic. Those should be banned when they have been identified as being unwholesome and unfit for human consumption!

Question:

I have a twenty-year-old daughter who I just found out is taking birth control pills. There are no medical reasons for her to be taking them. She does not know that I know about this. Should I confront her? How should I approach it?

Answer:

Yes, I would confront her. Hopefully you found out through legitimate channels and didn't resort to "snooping" into her personal belongings. This would indeed break her trust and confidence in you. There is a difference between dealing with a 20-year-old and a 10-year-old. Your greatest hope lies in the relationship you have already built with her through the years. I would not confront her with a condemning, hostile attitude. I would approach her with a great deal of love and concern. I wouldn't ask her pointed questions as to whether the reasons for the pills were for having sex. After all, at 20 years of age, if she wants to have sex, she will find a way, one way or another. Probing questions would only drive her to be more secretive. I would simply point out that premarital sex can be dangerous and leads to broken hearts, broken promises, and broken lives. Encourage her to talk with you or someone she respects who can give her good advice on this subject. Building a good relationship with her now is important. She is no longer a child so don't treat her as one. Make her know you are dealing with her as a responsible adult—responsible for her own actions.

Question:

Should babies born out of wedlock be al-

lowed to be taken to the altar and dedicated to the Lord just as legitimate babies?

Answer:

When Jesus called for the children to come to Him, He didn't say that He would receive only legitimate children. Illegitimate children aren't a new social category in this world! If any child needs the blessings of God, it would be such a child, for their heartaches and sorrows in life are just beginning. They need all the spiritual help they can receive to overcome the stigma that will always be attached to their conceptions. They did not ask to be born—legitimately or illegitimately. They should not have to bear the reproach of the sins of their parents. Yet our society assumes such an inhumane attitude. I would rather see the parents of an illegitimate child bring that child to the altar than to disregard the importance of God in their lives. It is our responsibility as spiritual people to use this child's dedication as a starting point to minister to that couple or that unwed mother or single father. They need to feel the love of Christians surrounding them. The major reason most girls get pregnant out of wedlock is not the result of sexual desires, but because they are looking for love and acceptance. They want to have something they can love. Jesus said that harlots and publicans would inherit the Kingdom of God before hypocrites and self-righteous people!

Question:

I have a teenager whom I must occasionally discipline. My philosophy of discipline at this age is to deprive him of something he really enjoys. One of the things he enjoys most is his

involvement in the church and the church school. Is it appropriate or wise to restrict his involvement in church or school activities as a form of punishment?

Answer:

You are correct in using things he enjoys as a form of discipline. But it is wrong to use the church as a form of punishment. We are responsible for the concepts of God our children hold. If He is pictured as a rod of correction, children will resent it. That correction is like sending a child to bed without food. We should never withhold any vital ingredient that is essential to healthy growth from our children as punishment. We don't tell our children not to brush their teeth as a punishment, or not take their medicine, or make them stay awake all night and give up sleep. Their spiritual well-being is just as important as all these natural areas. Children should be encouraged to participate in church and school activities. Withholding certain extracurricular activities may well be some areas you can evaluate as measures of discipline, if they are things that are not essential to character building.

Question:

We hear a great deal about child abuse today. Do you think there has really been a significant increase, or is it that we have become sensitive to the problem, and the obligation to report cases of abuse has brought more reports to authorities?

Answer:

I see a bumper sticker occasionally that says,

"It's alright to tell." I have mixed emotions about that message. It is one thing to create the atmosphere where a child will feel free to discuss problems, and quite another to alert them to the notion that every time their parents correct them, they are being abused. Even though it is the nature of children to exaggerate, we must take seriously any suspicious circumstances that may indicate there is child abuse. It is natural for children to resent correction. If they are told they can have their parents punished for correcting them, children will tell. This can be disastrous. I'm not sure there is that much more child abuse today than there has always been; I do know there has been much more reporting of it because our society has been sensitized toward it. I heard the other day there was a move afoot to ban any kind of spanking or corporal punishment by parents on the grounds it is abusive. This would be another example of government intrusion into our private lives. I am fully aware there is abuse and there are those who abuse children. This is sometimes obvious to teachers, neighbors, other family members and other associates. By law, teachers or anyone who deals with children must report even "suspected" child abuse. We comply with this law. But underlying this whole situation, I see the subtle hand of Satan trying to break down the authority of the family and fragment the home.

Question:

I know a lady who sucked her thumb when she was small. Now, her mouth bears the obvious disfigurement of those who suck their thumbs. She, however, thinks it is cute when her own child sucks her thumb and will take no

action to stop it. Is she doing her child a per-manent disservice?

Answer:

Most parents want their children to be spared the problems, disadvantages, and heartbreaks that the parents have known. For example, my dad was not able to get an education, and what education he did get was by having my mother read to him by the light of a lantern at night. He had to work in the fields all day. As the more fortunate children walked to school past the fields where he plowed, he would stand and cry, longing to be able to go to school with them. He purposed in his heart then and there that if he ever had children, he would see to it that they had an education. He kept that promise. One of his great-est pleasures was the knowledge that his children all received good educations. Even so, you would think a mother could look in the mirror and see the obvious signs of a thumb-sucker, and purpose not to have that impediment inflicted on the features of her own daughter. It's almost as if she revels in the mistake she made and wishes to see her daughter make the same mistake. If she would receive gentle advice from a friend, that advice would be to take whatever steps necessary to keep that from happening to her own child. Proven methods will remedy this condi-tion. She ought to act while there is still time. Hope-fully, what she is doing will not be permanent.

Question:

My parents not only try to tell me how to control and discipline my children, but when-ever the opportunity avails itself, they take it upon themselves to do the correcting. This goes

beyond normal grandparents' control. How should I deal with it?

Answer:

God's plan is for parents to raise their own children. Grandparents, however well-intentioned they may be, often spoil their grandchildren. They feel the same love they had for their children, but perhaps time has dulled their keen understanding that permissiveness will ruin a child. On the other hand, there are those grandparents who take charge and try to discipline grandchildren. Any discipline they administer should always be with the approval of the parents. Children innately seek to have their own way. They will play one adult against the other to get what they want. Don't allow that manipulation to happen. Parents and grandparents should come into agreement over their discipline. If you haven't discussed this with your parents, you should do so calmly and without condemning them. Express your appreciation for their interest, but suggest they coordinate their discipline with yours. And remember, they are still your parents, and you never cease honoring them.

Question:

I am a 15-year-old girl. When my mom gets angry with me or I do something she doesn't approve, she slaps me in the face. I deeply resent this. In the first place, is she right in doing this? And secondly, what can I do about it?

Answer:

I would advise the mother that even though she

recognizes the need for correction, slapping in the face is never an appropriate discipline. There are certain areas of the body that receive correction more receptively than others. For some reason, to slap someone in the face denotes an insult. We do not want to insult our children; we want to correct them. If physical means are necessary, paddling is far better suited for correction than slapping. A slap in the face usually precipitates a hostile response. It is said that Fulton, the inventor of the steam boat, concluded that to get the best results, it is always better to paddle from the rear! As for the young lady, I would hope that you receive whatever correction is given to you with a spirit of love. Perhaps the example Jesus demonstrated when they slapped Him would be one to follow . . . "forgive them, for they know not what they do." Your mother may indeed know that a correction is needed, but she doesn't know how to administer it appropriately. Perhaps you could discuss it with her calmly with an attitude of love and understanding. Suggest to her that you realize you need correction, but that the results might be better if she used another method. If you feel the abuse is too severe, you should discuss it with your pastor, a school official or even a physician.

FOUR

How Do I Know
When I'm Hooked?

C an I become addicted to my prescription drugs? I know some people who deal in drugs. Should I report them and risk getting involved and hurt? What about someone doing drugs in front of their kids? What's the difference in being addicted to alcohol and pot?

The curse of our age is drugs. It has caused the destruction of many homes and lives. Here are some tough questions and answers. Maybe they will help . . .

Question:

Since many people use what we call legal or prescription drugs, when is the use of these drugs wrong or sinful, even though they may be legal according to the law?

Answer:

Just because something may be legal does not mean it is not sinful. The Bible instructs us not to defile the "temple of God" or our bodies. There are those times where certain drugs aid in our healing and recovery. But for the most part, these drugs will be administered under the direction and care of a physician. But when we become dependent or addicted to any substance, we have allowed something to defile our bodies. Many drugs, such as antibiotics, etc., have little or no effect on our mental state. But when we become dependent upon mind-altering drugs or drugs that adjust our behavior and mood, then we open ourselves for spirits to enter our lives. So, the criteria of the use of drugs is not whether or not they are legal or even totally under the final decision of a physician. It is whenever we realize we are becoming addicted or dependent on a drug, or we recognize that the drug is changing our responses, character or personality for the worse.

Question:

My ex-husband has a drug habit. He has visitation rights with our children. When they are with him, they witness his use of drugs. I try not to say negative things about their father to them, but now they are beginning to ask questions about what is going on. What should my

response be and what should I do about the situation?

Answer:

The courts often revoke visitation rights if children are abused. This clearly could become an abusive situation. You might discuss these visits with the proper authorities and inform them of the details. The problem, however, is always the children. He is their father, and they love him. You are correct in not demeaning his character to them. Even though you should not talk about him, you do have the responsibility to teach them that drug use is wrong and illegal and leads to much heartache and sorrow. If they ask about their father, I would suggest to them that they pray for him, continue in their love for him, but realize that he is a person with a problem who needs help. I assume you have tried to discuss their questions with your ex-husband in a civil way without arguing. If not, perhaps you could calmly tell him that the children were upset with what was going on. It might cause him to seek help.

Question:

I strongly suspect that my teenager is experimenting with drugs. I know that kids can always slip and do things if they really want to because we can't monitor their every move. What is the best way for me to deal with the situation without driving him into doing something reckless?

Answer:

To ignore a problem and just assume that all young people must experiment with danger and "sow their wild oats" can be costly. First of all, Christian training is important. Making sure they go to church during these early impressionable years should not be an option, but a necessity. We don't ask our kids whether they want to go to school, take baths, go to the doctor, etc. Why then should we ask them if they want to go to church? Too often we wait until a problem explodes and then we try to remedy the situation. "Remember thy Creator in the days of thy youth BEFORE the evil day comes" is the admonition of the Bible.

If you suspect your teen is using drugs, learn all the syptoms of drug use—drastic change of lifestyle, new and mysterious friends, listlessness, dropping grades, poor personal appearance, and others you can learn from numerous sources. Then if you are still convinced he is experimenting with drugs, I would think you should calmly confront him about it. I would do so from the standpoint of trying to see that he understands the destructive consequences to his body and his life. Don't approach him from the standpoint of wanting to punish him for disobeying you. Try to show your great love and concern, not your wrath and judgment. Also, don't hesitate to get spiritual and professional input from ministers, doctors and others who deal with addictive behavior regularly.

Question:

Before I became a Christian, I was involved with people who sold drugs. After ending that association, I went to the police and told them everything I knew about their operation, yet the police have not been able to arrest them. These people are also involved in witchcraft.

They have threatened to use it on me because I "ratted" on them. What should I do?

Answer:

If you have reported their threats to the authorities and still have reason to believe that you are in physical danger, I would contact whatever other police agencies who might render assistance like the DEA (Drug Enforcement Agency) and explain the circumstances and seek their protection. As far as witchcraft is concerned, if you are a Christian, you seek the divine covering and protection of the Holy Spirit. "Greater is He that is within us than he that is in the world . . ." You might want to share it with your pastor and allow him and other intercessors to join you in prayer that God will bind and destroy those evil spirits that control these people. Also, pray for them that despitefully use you. If these were former friends, wouldn't it be wonderful for them to see the power of God in your life and turn from their wicked ways because of your testimony? Finally, read and live out the protection of God through His covenants described in Psalm 91.

Question:

I am a teenaged boy. I don't do any type of drugs, but my dad constantly harps on all "drug-head" kids. He does this while a cigarette droops from his lips and he is holding his beer can. I really want to respect him as my father. Yet I am having a hard time dealing with this obvious inconsistency. Am I right that addiction is addiction, regardless of your age and regardless of whether it is "pot" or beer or cigarettes. What do you think?

Answer:

First, you should respect and honor your father. This is a spiritual commandment. But you have pinpointed a severe problem within our society. Addiction is addiction, whatever name it goes by. Nicotine, alcohol, all these are addictive substances. And you are right, it is a little like the "pot calling the kettle black." But it is not your place to correct your father. Show him love and allow your Christian witness to minister to him. Don't argue with him. If he should enter into a discussion with you about the subject, then you should respond very calmly and objectively without pointing out his particular error. Deal with principles in your discussion rather than specifics. No father likes to think his child is correcting him. However, if he sees your maturity, it may have an effect on him, and the day may well come when he will ask for your input to his own situation. Then, you can respond in love and kindness, showing him the need to deal with his own dependency upon these substances. In addition, you might find great help by attending a church or neighborhood self-help group to support you and assist you in dealing with your father's substance abuse.

FIVE

It Is My Money,
Isn't It?

Do I tithe off my gross or net income? Do I tithe first or after I pay my bills? What is the difference in tithing to a church and giving to charity? I pay my tithes regularly, yet I still have financial problems. Whatever happened to the "prosperity" gospel?

Stewardship over our money is an important item. Here are some things you should know about covenant . . .

Question:

My mother is in her sixties and cannot work anymore. She has very little financial resources. I feel some responsibility for her welfare. My husband's parents were able to save money during their working years. Because they need no financial help from us, he says that it is not our place to give my mother any money either. Do children have any responsibilities to care for their aged parents financially?

Answer:

In my opinion we are never relieved of our responsibilities for our families, both our children after us or our parents before us. Old age robs us of our ability to care for ourselves. We must remember those days they cared for us when we were helpless. One of the most traumatic experiences of my life is watching the physical and mental deterioration of my own parents. I feel it is the least I can do, along with my brother and sisters, to see that they are cared for as long as they live. If parents have savings and need no help, that is wonderful. But if they are helpless and cannot work, they become the responsibility of their children. We must always remember the cycle of life. We, too, someday may be helpless and need the assistance of our children.

Question:

If you get behind on paying your tithes, is it appropriate to catch up or should you just pick up wherever you left off? Will God hold you responsible for the tithes you did not pay?

Answer:

In the Old Testament, any tithe that was with-held had to be paid back with interest. This was under the dispensation of the Law. When we come to the New Testament, tithing is not only a require-ment, but also becomes an expression of our spiritual commitment to God and understanding of covenant. It is no longer an exercise of the law, but it becomes a matter of the heart. Getting behind in our tithing reflects a lapse in our covenant. If we make nothing, then we pay nothing. However, if we do make some-thing, the tithe should be given to God first—the first fruit. The New Testament gives us a higher concept of tithing. In the Old Testament, the tithe was a tenth of all income. In the New Testament we are taught to give "as the Lord has prospered us." The Apostle Paul in II Corinthians 9 teaches us to "pur-pose in our hearts" to give unto the Lord cheerfully. Just as there are other forms of worship, giving is an act of worship. Even as we also need to worship regu-larly, we need to give to God regularly.

Question:

Should tithe be paid "off the top" or after all other bills are paid?

Answer:

God said to "seek ye first the Kingdom of God and His righteousness and these other things will be added unto you." Even so, God expects to receive our first effort. "Thou shalt have no other Gods before me" is a commandment of God. If we consider any obligation more important than our obligation to God, it then becomes a priority or "god" in our lives. This was the first sin of Cain's. While Abel gave his best, the first fruit, Cain gave what was left. God looks not only at the gift, but also at the attitude of the giver.

Question:
Do you tithe off of your gross or net income?

Answer:
God doesn't count pennies. He is concerned with the attitude of our giving. God actually doesn't need our money. He needs us and our resources to accomplish the mission of His Kingdom. Gross income indicates all money that passes through our hands. There are some businesses that do not know what their gross income will be until the end of a fiscal year. In some cases, people pay tithes on their net income until they know what the gross income is. If we rationalize that we should pay our tithe on what is left after we meet our other obligations, then we do exactly what Cain did. Tithe is a "first fruit" which indicates to me that it comes from the gross income.

Question:
If you attend this church and your spouse is a member elsewhere, do you divide the tithes between the two churches?

Answer:
In the first place, it seems that there is an "unequal yoking" here. Even though both a husband and a wife may profess to be Christians, I would hope they would at some point come to an understanding and agreement on a single place of worship. You seem to be walking in the same direction on two different roads. I don't think such an arrangement

will survive in the long run. Usually I suggest that the tithe go to the church where one of the spouses is more involved. If both are equally involved, then perhaps dividing the tithe is a temporary solution. But the permanent solution is walking the same road together.

Question:

If you contribute to a worthy charitable organization, can you count this as your tithe?

Answer:

Tithe and charitable giving are two different contributions. Charitable giving is good, but it does not suffice for tithing. The Bible speaks of tithing and it speaks of "almsgiving." Almsgiving is "sowing precious seed" to create an atmosphere of a good harvest. Responsible Christians sow into many religious and charitable causes. But God's plan to finance the work of His Church is the tithing system.

Question:

I was raised in a "New Age" religion. The word "prosperity" was always used in reference to an abundance of material things—cars, houses, etc. I grew up thinking that "seed planting" was an investment. You plant a little, and you get a lot back. Because of this conditioning, it is difficult for me to understand and relate to the proper attitude to spiritual giving. Could you please give me insight on how I can overcome this?

Answer:

We do not plant seed in order to reap a material

harvest. Spiritual "seed planting" has to do with eternal harvest or reaping spiritual rewards. Reaping benefits of "seed planting" can be in good health, good relationships, and other areas of quality living. It does not always translate into dollars and cents. If this is what we do it for, we have missed the point.

Question:
I have legal guardianship over an elderly family member who has been declared incompetent in handling his financial affairs. Do I have the legal right or spiritual right to tithe, give alms and offerings on this money?

Answer:
As long as the family member lives, you should tithe only on that which may be yours legally. For example, most executors receive a fee or a percentage for their stewardship. This serves as income to you and should be tithed upon. However, if other family members unanimously agree with you that the estate should be tithed upon, and there are no legal stipulations prohibiting it, then you could do so. After the family member is deceased and you have the final and full responsibility to make all financial decisions, in my opinion you have the right to tithe on the estate or give alms by planting precious seed into the spiritual harvest.

Question:
We have been faithful in our covenant with God to the very best of our ability. We pay our tithes, give seed faith offerings, special offerings to the building fund and any other special requests that come from our spiritual leaders.

We are not extravagant in our lifestyles and we cut every corner possible to make ends meet. We even try to rejoice in our warfare. Yet it seems every time we start to get ahead, we are hit by an unexpected major expense. What encouragement or advice could you give us?

Answer:

Often the greater the work you do in the Kingdom of God, the greater the warfare that surrounds you. Jesus told a story of a poor man, Lazarus, who had nothing of this world's goods. But when he went home to Father Abraham's bosom, he had the eternal riches of God. A rich man who had ignored Lazarus' plight and who fared sumptuously and lacked for nothing in this life also died. But in "torments" he lifted up his eyes and pleaded for Lazarus to come bring him one drop of water. A graphic story! Many Christians do enjoy prosperity. But financial prosperity is not guaranteed. In this life we often reap our rewards in other ways. Our reward is in eternal values. My advice is to bear the hardship as a good soldier and to trust God. He did promise to meet our needs. Victory lies in the eternal realm.

Six

Are You Telling Me The Truth, Doc?

I'm overweight. What about all these diets? How does a Christian take care of his body? Why are some people sicker than others? Is it spiritual warfare? What about divine healing . . . is it really possible? If a person can't bear the pain and commits suicide, is it an unforgivable sin?

Our bodies are the "temples" of the Holy Spirit. How we treat them is important. Here are some important guidelines that will give you direction . . .

Question:

In Genesis 6:3 it states that God has given man a life span of 120 years. In another place it says 3 score and 10, which is 70 years. Please explain the 50 year differential.

Answer:

What we should realize is that even the Psalmist was subjected to discouragement. On the day he penned the 3 score and 10, he was obviously "in the pits." He went on to say that even if man's days should be seventy years, those days would be filled with heartache and sorrow. Many people took these words as a mandate for the life span of man. The promise of life, however, is found in Genesis which states that man's life span can be 120 years. It is interesting that recently a scientific report that was not intended to support this scriptural claim said that man's body, if well cared for, could feasibly live 120 years!

Question:

When I hear a message preached on divine healing, many people come to mind from the past—good people who were not healed, and who died premature deaths in the prime of their lives. I've been battling a disease for 14 years, have had 4 operations and have endured a number of treatments, but to no avail. I was raised Pentecostal, and can quote all the "name it, claim it, frame it" scriptures. It is so easy to condemn yourself and at the same time question God when you are not healed when you are begging for healing. When you hear divine healing preached, it sounds so simple. Why isn't

it?

Answer:

With our mortal, finite eyes we see, at best, only a small portion of God's ultimate plan for our lives. The steps of the righteous are directed by the Lord. If we commit our way to Him, He will direct our paths. We must always be aware of the fact that we are eternal creatures, and this earthly life is but a fragment of time. The soul and being of a man will never die. It changes dimensions through physical death. That will happen to all of us.

Certain physical and natural laws are in effect for all of us. Sickness and death claim the righteous as well as the wicked. The difference is, the righteous know eternal life, while the wicked shall be accorded spiritual and eternal death and separation from God and His goodness for all eternity. Romans 8:28 says that all things work for good to them who love the Lord and are called to His purposes. Even though we may not understand moments of suffering, if we believe the Word of God, we must believe that everything that happens to us works for our ultimate redemption, both physically and spiritually. The estate of sin into which we all were born is responsible for sickness and suffering. It is possible to live an "abundant life" in the midst of suffering. But even "abundant life" may include physical suffering. Through our suffering we often serve a higher purpose and witness to those who observe us in our patience. We are told that in our patience, we possess our souls . . . our eternal man. Though the outward, physical man perishes, the inward soul of man is renewed day by day.

It is natural to ask the question, "Why?" You

should not condemn yourself for these natural responses. The important thing is finally to realize our lives are in the hands of God. He is wise, just and compassionate. He will not allow us to be tempted or to suffer beyond that which we can bear and will with our temptation and our suffering make a way of escape. Healing comes by faith, not our worthiness. By His stripes we were healed. Healing does not come to us because we may be righteous. It is by the suffering of Christ that we receive healing. Not all healing is physical. God knows what kind of healing is necessary for us in order to bring us to a deeper understanding of His purposes for our lives.

Question:

A friend of mine has a disease which though not immediately terminal, brings much constant agony. There is no relief that medicine can bring. He has prayed for divine healing, and he has committed it to the will of God. Sometimes the pain is so excruciating he can hardly bear it and would rather be dead. My question: Some countries allow people who are terminally ill with great pain and suffering to end their lives in dignity and with medical supervision. Is this an unforgivable sin? Would a Christian who felt this was their only recourse be sent to hell by a loving and wise God?

Answer:

There is in my interpretation of Scripture no approval given for the taking of life in this situation, either by someone else or by the person himself. It would then be interpreted as being a sin. Your question was would it be an "unforgivable" sin. The Bible only speaks of one such sin and that is blasphemy against the Holy Spirit. My greatest source of consolation is that God is an all-wise, all-knowing, compassionate God. The Bible says that He will not suffer us to be tempted above that which we are able to bear but will with the temptation make a way of escape. I have to believe that even in this situation, God will provide that way of escape. God didn't say what "that way" would be. I am sure it is different according to the individual's ability and capacity to bear the temptation. The important issue is that we must trust a God who is good.

Question:

Women with large breasts seem to be very fashionable these days. Many women with small breasts seem to feel inferior. Therefore, many women are having mammary augmentations in order to enhance their appearance. What is your opinion on this? Is it a spiritual matter?

Answer:

There are several considerations to be made here. First of all, the motive. Is this surgery motivated by vanity? Where will it lead? Will liposuction be next? Then a tummy tuck? Then a face lift perhaps? Self-image is important. If a woman feels inferior because of small or non-existent breasts and augmentation is medically suggested and mutually agreed upon by both partners in the marriage, then there is nothing sinful, as such. However, information is now coming in that these augmentations can cause unforeseen problems and often have to be redone or removed after a number of years. The introduction of any foreign substance into the body can often cause reactions. Again, the motive and where it ultimately can lead is the key. Priority is also a consideration. These procedures can be very costly and time consuming. So, even though they may not be sinful, every ingredient and far-reaching ramification should be considered and agreed upon by both husband and wife before acting.

Question:
If God grants a person rights over his own body, why is suicide considered a sin?

Answer:
God created life and it is sacred to Him. He said, "Thou shalt not kill." Suicide is killing life which is a sin. It is probably a misconception when we say we have "rights" over our body. The body is described as the "temple of the Holy Spirit." The "right" we have over our body is to protect it, care for it, but most of all, present it as a "living" sacrifice to God. God does not require our bodies as dead sacrifices. Suicide is a cruel act. It solves no problems, but creates many for those who are left behind, especially children.

Question:
Many diets are in vogue today. Some of them emphasize opposite techniques in order to accomplish the same thing—losing weight. What is the most effective and even spiritual way to lose weight?

Answer:
Fads won't last. If a person is losing weight to get into this year's swimsuit, when summer is gone, all the weight will return. You must be convinced

first that losing weight is a matter of good health, and that it should be an ongoing concept. Vanity is not the right motivation. The desire to have a proper appearance is a different motivation from vanity. Motives are important in all that we do.

Diet should be a disciplined lifestyle. Metabolism differences account for weight gain differences in many people. Though some claim they "have glandular problems," most experts agree that is not considered a legitimate medical reason for weight gain. Many people are simply compulsive eaters. They eat when they are lonely, angry, anxious, bored and other reasons than being hungry or actually needing food. The only way to lose weight and leave it off is to develop a disciplined lifestyle. As we grow older there is usually a tendency to gain weight. We should adjust our eating habits as we grow older. We should get proper physical exercise for our bodies. Caring for our bodies is indeed a spiritual exercise also. We should seek the strength of the Holy Spirit to come against compulsions to eat which can be very addictive. You might consider Christian support groups which provide help in dealing with compulsive eating.

Question:
Why do some families seem to have more physical sickness than others? Is it possible they are leaving the door open to Satan to enter through sickness to discourage them? Is this a form of "spiritual warfare?"

Answer:
Satan always attempts to thwart the plan of God. God implements His plans through people, and often through families. The house of Levi show God's

use of families for His service. Satan does attempt to destroy the "seed." The account of Moses is an example. Satan tried to destroy the seed of God. Herod sought to destroy the seed of God, Jesus Christ. Satan is also aware that nothing can be quite as discouraging as chronic sickness in our families and especially with our children. To those families God has given an anointing and power to withstand this warfare over the family.

Question:
If you have received prayer for a physical healing, does continuing to take prescribed drugs indicate your lack of faith?

Answer:
Healing from God takes many forms. He has provided one form of healing within the body itself. When we cut ourselves, nature begins the healing process by coagulating the blood to stop the bleeding. Antibodies within the system are activated to thwart infection. This process is built-in and is a form of divine healing. God's miraculous intervention is also a form of divine healing. This is when God directly intervenes. Perhaps a person's ability to recover naturally is inoperative, or in cases of physical impairments, beyond medical help. God can and does miraculously, instantaneously heal. But yet another form of healing is provided through doctors and medicines. Medicines, for the most part, are derived from herbs, plants, etc., that come from God's ground. God provided healing through these provisions of His earth. God gave man the knowledge to understand these processes, and they can be used for healing purposes. The improper use of drugs is wrong. Drugs

are improperly used to the point of addiction or for the wrong motives. As in other areas, those things used for good can also be used for evil. A car can transport a murderer or a preacher. Being under the care of a competent physician does not denote a lack of faith. In fact, if there is a miraculous healing, it is appropriate for a physician to confirm that healing.

SEVEN

Is Uncle Sam
Too Powerful Today?

I s government intrusion in our private lives a problem today? What about separation of Church and state? I'm an activist. Should I be nonviolent or be prepared to use force if necessary to get the job done? What about our welfare system? Is it working in our society? Is the death penalty scriptural? What about people suing the Church? What about the right to life? What about the right to die? There is a role that government should play in our lives.

Any time this church speaks out on an issue, it pleases some and displeases others. Our main concern is not to be men pleasers, but to do and speak the will of God. We have made statements about abortion and I fear our intentions have not been fully heard. We know that we are not going to please both camps, the pro-life and the pro-choice groups.

But I do have some concerns that go beyond the obvious issue of the life of unborn babies. I must be concerned with other issues that surround the central issue, for they too are very important. For instance, one of my major concerns is the growing tendency of the government to regulate our private lives. I do understand the responsibility of government to protect the innocent. I do know that government should reflect morality in its laws. But the fact remains, we are happy if they enforce "our" side of the issue. But suppose they enforce the "other" side of the issue? Do we still want government intervention then? You say, that's the reason we are in the streets, to get the right laws passed. I maintain it is possible for me as a spiritual leader to have more influence talking with the senators, the speakers of the house and even presidents than to spend my time in jail proving my point.

Some have reminded us that we walked the picket line during the civil rights struggle at supermarkets. Yes, we did. But in my mind here is the difference. If a person comes to the store to buy groceries and is faced with the prospect of having to cross or honor a picket line in order to buy a quart of milk it is not a traumatic decision to make. But consider a frightened fifteen-year-old unwed mother already traumatized by her situation looking for a way out of her dilemma. I can't and don't justify her actions, but I still love her. And while there are those who stand on picket lines who wouldn't lift a finger to hurt her but only want to help her, I have seen others who scream "murderer" at her, further traumatizing her. I see the same spirit in some of their eyes that was in the eyes of those who dragged the woman to Jesus accusing her of adultery and demanding she be stoned to death. And with Jesus I say to those who accuse, let those who are without sin cast the first stone. Would you have me believe it is right to sacrifice her life for the life of her baby? Jesus Christ did that on the cross. He gave His life for our sins. We don't practice sacrificing one life for another after Christ made the ultimate sacrifice. The question is, how do we effectively deal with this problem today?

As a spiritual leader in this community, my role is to get to the source of the problem and what causes this young girl to be in this predicament. An unhappy home, parents who neglected her, poverty, ignorance —these are issues the church must address.

Those who feel their convictions mandate that they stand personally on a picket line have my greatest admiration. I respect their convictions and uphold their right to express their convictions. But I add, please do it in a Christian manner. Screaming at and taunting already devastated girls in my opinion is not what Jesus Christ is all about. I think He would have ministered to her, showed her compassion and told her to go and sin no more.

Some have called for "open discussion and debate" on this issue in our church. My policy is that God has given me the charge and care of this sheepfold. I try as much as is humanly possible to please all the people while doing the will of God. But I will not allow any service we have to degrade into a public shouting match like a Geraldo or Ophra Winfrey show. That never solves the problem. What we need to do is seek the face of God for power to eradicate the reason this tragedy exists in the first place. I simply say though government has a role to enforce the will of the majority of the people in a free, democratic society, the government is not the solution to the problem. By enforcing the will of the majority, this does not ensure that what they enforce is right. The Bible says the path is broad that leads to destruction and many—the majority—travel that road. The road that leads to eternal life is narrow and few—the minority will find it. The real question I would ask you is do you believe in democracy or theocracy? They are not the same. Democracy adheres to the will of the people. Theocracy adheres to the will of God.

And those who may perceive that they would be "blackballed" by spiritual authority for expressing dissent or concern don't really understand me. I claim no papal infallibility. This ministry, on the contrary, was built out of personal tragedy. But personal tragedy also taught me some hard lessons about forgiveness and compassion. My advice before you cast your first stone at anyone: place yourself, or your fifteen-year-old daughter in their shoes. You may see it differently then . . .

Question:
What role should the government play in determining moral issues in our society?

Answer:
The role of the government in our lives should be to serve the people. Elected officials are as indicated, "public servants". Perhaps they have lost this perspective and feel the reverse is true. This is what has happened in countries that have degenerated into totalitarian states. The role of the citizen is to serve

the state. This is especially characteristic of communist countries. An interesting current observation is that Eastern Europe and the Baltic countries and even Russia itself are being forced by public pressure verging upon revolution to move back toward a more democratic and open society. Meanwhile, we here in the United States of America seem to be moving toward more and more government controls.

Though the government has the responsibility to protect the citizens, it is in my opinion the responsibility of the Church to establish moral standards. Obviously, the laws of the land should reflect those established standards. For example, the government says it is unlawful to pray in schools. That means any type of religious expression is forbidden in order to "protect the rights" of a few dissenters. Democracy implies that the will of the majority prevails. We now, however, are being ruled by the will of a few dissenters. What we are seeing today is more and more government intrusion in not only religious freedoms, but also in our personal lives. The role of the government is to create a base broad enough so as to include the freedom of all forms of religious expression and to protect those rights and freedoms. We have seen the reverse in this country. The government has taken on the role of an oppressor of religion. In my spiritual judgment, increasing government control is a satanic ploy to destroy the influence of God and the Church in this nation. The Congress of the United States, local legislatures and even local municipalities should be sensitive to the Church universal and mandate that the laws of the land reflect moral interpretations of the religious community. Laws would not necessarily reflect theological premises. The Ten Commandments, if adhered to, would create a good basis for any society—protection of life, limb and property. There are other dogmas in other religions that reflect the higher values of man. If there are those religions which feel it is their responsibility and mission to literally destroy those who do not agree with them, then obviously they violate not only the laws of God but universal concepts of decency, dignity and human rights. The government has a right to address this. But the government should not set theological precedents through legislation.

Question:
What role should the government play in the abortion issue?

Answer:
Whether or not abortion is murder is open to many interpretations. There are many self-proclaimed "experts" in the field. The issue we should consider first is the character of God and what He desires. Is the interruption of a pregnancy for medical purposes to save the life of a mother murder? How would some explain the very concept of Jesus Christ giving His life in order that others might live? Did God "murder" Jesus Christ? Was He indeed the "Lamb slain from the foundation of the world?" All of these are deep theological questions that secular courts and legislators are not qualified to answer. Every situation is different and merits consideration. For instance, what do you do with a 12-year-old Mongoloid child who is raped by a senile grandfather (an actual case)? Should her ability to become a mother while a child herself be a consideration? Some would exchange or sacrifice her life for an unborn fetus. These

are very heavy questions that divide the church today. They are decisions that should be made by the families involved with the input of medical authorities and spiritual advisors. It is not the role of the government to make these decisions. I seriously question government support of abortion. The government should enforce the will of the people while the role of the Church is to influence the moral judgment of the people.

Question:
Is capital punishment—legally putting criminals to death—scripturally right or wrong?

Answer:
In the Old Testament criminals were put to death. The Bible says the law is for the lawless. However, the New Testament fulfilled the law and brought the age of grace and forgiveness. But even then, the Bible plainly says that grace was not given in order for sin, or crime in this case, to abound. In the case of the state taking a life, there is always the possibility of an innocent person wrongly charged and punished. For that reason, the procedure should be thorough to ensure that the innocent are protected. However, what we see much of the time are obvious guilty criminals being released on technicalities. There has to be some safeguard against this. To answer the question specifically about scriptural basis, the Old Testament would seem to support capital punishment. "An eye for an eye and a tooth for a tooth." The New Testament introduces grace and forgiveness as a factor. Yet, when our children violate our rules, we may forgive them, but we still discipline and correct them, for we realize if they go

without correction, they will likely violate the rules again.

I think the government has a right and an obligation to protect society against proven violent men. We are talking about putting to death people who have violently killed other people and have been legally convicted. Even though the government has the right to do this, it is still a question we must answer in our hearts. I would ask a person who does not believe in capital punishment to do this: imagine your wife, daughter, son, mother or some one very dear to you is senselessly slaughtered by someone. The murderer is apprehended and convicted. Would you still want to run the risk of their being back out on the streets in seven years? You may even forgive them for what they did, but would you want to run the risk that they might do the same thing again? So, as Jesus often did, I answered a question with a question!

Question:

What would be your view on the death penalty if the victim was your daughter or the criminal on death row was your son? Would you feel the same way both ways about capital punishment?

Answer:

If my son was guilty, I still would not change my mind. In the natural because I am his father and I love him dearly I would hope and pray for clemency. Because of my love for him, I would probably die of grief. But if I knew that he was indeed guilty, then I would not blame the state for enforcing the law. He would have to pay the penalty described by law for his crime. I can't change that fact. What I would realize is that I had failed as a father when he was younger. The Bible says to train up a child in the way he should go, and when he is old he will not depart from those truths. Obviously I failed to instill these truths in him, so now I must live with the guilt and knowledge of my own failure and realize I played a role in putting him to death.

Question:
Do you think the Supreme Court has overstepped its boundaries of authority in this country?

Answer:
Yes, I think the Supreme Court as well as the legislative branch and in some cases the executive branch have overstepped their boundaries of authority. They do not perceive themselves as servants of the people, but as masters of the people. They do not perceive themselves as protectors of the peoples' freedoms but as interpreters of what freedoms are appropriate for the people to enjoy. The court is divided into camps of the "liberals" and "conservatives." This is an indication that personal interpretations are brought to bear in their decisions. Decisions ought to be made on the basis of the good of all the people, not on some political affiliation. The justices are appointed for life. They have no one to whom they must answer. The remote possibility of impeachment exists, but the judges realize impeachment is so rare that it is little deterrent for their making their decisions based on their own interpretations. I personally believe that if the founders and framers of this country could see what is taking place in our

society with our government and our courts, they would be sorely disappointed!

Question:

Should the laws of the land reflect the moral standards set by the Church, or should government take a lead in passing laws that bring about high moral standards?

Answer:

It is absolutely the responsibility of the Church to take the lead in setting and interpreting moral standards. It is the role of the government to reflect these standards in its application of the law, not necessarily by enforcing stringent laws, but rather by insuring the freedoms of the Church to establish guidelines that are ethical and moral. For example, we believe in the right to life. But we acknowledge that there are always extenuating circumstances. If the government passes a law concerning life either way, they interfere with the Church in setting its standards. If they say abortion is illegal, they force children to have babies they cannot care for, mothers' lives to be threatened, etc. If they say abortion is legal, they give tacit approval to illicit sex and promiscuousness by providing abortion as a means of birth control. They cause hundreds of fetuses to be destroyed, and along with them, the possibility of a productive life. In my opinion, the Church should take the lead in establishing moral and ethical standards with the protected freedom to do so. Individuals must respond voluntarily. The Church cannot force its views on people. Then a person must answer to a higher court than the Supreme Court— the Supreme Being.

Question:

In a time when many other countries are returning to the concepts of democracy as a form of government, why is it that America is going in the opposite direction and becoming more and more repressive of personal and religious freedoms?

Answer:

Some have said that democracy is its own worst enemy. It allows dissenters to speak their peace through freedom of speech. But somewhere along the line, we confused the right of a person to speak freely as their lawful right if it were not for the good of the people. For the most part, this country is run by bureaucrats who are either hired or appointed and have no direct responsibility to the electorate. These are people who often have jaundiced views toward the Church, the freedom of people, true democracy, the personal rights of people, etc. They make arbitrary decisions that effect everyone, and they do not have to answer for them to the people. The most powerful agency in this country is the IRS who has little or no controls by the people. If left unchecked, they will become the greatest enemy to the organized Church in this country. That is a prophecy! Gradually, by acquiescence we are losing our personal and corporate freedoms and are moving toward a state-controlled society. Hopefully we won't have to learn the hard lesson that Eastern Europe and other countries have had to learn in order to protect our precious freedoms.

Question:

Please explain your view of the conflict

between the Jews and the Arabs and their
ongoing war. Who is God really behind in this
situation?

Answer:

This war began with Isaac and Ishmael. Read
the story in the Bible for the background. Both were
the sons of Abraham, but Ishmael and his mother
Hagar were put out to fend for themselves. The whole
incident was because of disobedience to God and His
plan. Through the centuries there has been conflict
between the Arabs (Ishmael) and Jews (Isaac). God
looks on and is saddened by the fact that brothers
cannot agree. He loves both of them, and His will is
that they live together in harmony and peace. Ba-
sically, they fight over the land and of one dispos-
sessing the other of his land. A person skilled with
Scripture and history could take either side and make
a credible presentation. In my opinion we have
missed the whole point. The point is restoration and
forgiveness and brotherhood. God must look down
and see us as children fighting over a toy, each
screaming and kicking yelling that it is his! God is
not behind anyone who uses violence to prove his
point. God is love—and we do not see the character of
God in this conflict.

Question:

I am an activist for many worthy causes—
conservation, nuclear disarmament, Amnesty
International, holistic medicine, Greenpeace,
etc. I feel Scripture mandates our involvement
in these issues as concerned and responsible
Christians. My question is: what are Christians' guidelines for civil disobedience, and in

some cases breaking immoral laws to draw
attention to injustice and to get unjust laws
changed or repealed?

Answer:

At Chapel Hill we have endeavored to increase
our awareness of social and political evils. We are
attempting to address the ills of society wherever we
can. Obviously, it is a tremendous task and it will
take great effort to see results. As in the civil rights
movement, social and civil disobedience sometimes
becomes necessary. Civil disobedience becomes necessary after every possible legal method has been
tried and exhausted. God is never in favor of violence. I have often been surprised by the hostility of
both pro-lifers and pro-choice advocates. They seem
to lose the original point. They seem to want to fight
for the sake of fighting. There is a difference in being
a "professional activists" who just enjoys the rigors
of battle and the machinations and maneuvering of a
person who acts out of a genuine concern and conviction. I admire the person who is willing to die for his
convictions, but I have problems with those who are
obviously headline-hunting. Whenever you dissent,
ask yourself what your real motive is before you hit
the picket line.

Question:

I am a black man who is the father of several children. I love my family very much and
want to support them. Because of my circumstances, I cannot make enough money to support them at this time. The only way I can get
government help for them is not to live with
them. Then the government will give my family

food stamps and welfare. Even though I don't want to, the only way to get help is to move out. What is the answer?

Answer:

You are the victim of a system that perpetuates this problem. The government has not come up with a suitable answer for distributing aid to people who really need it the most. The welfare system is a classic case of misplaced priorities in our government. Many black men have been disenfranchised and have been emasculated emotionally by this system. Whenever possible, the Church should try to aid in reclaiming the pride and dignity of all men, especially black men in this situation. But my specific answer as to what you should do is to maintain as close a relationship with your family as possible. If you are truly in covenant with God and stand on His promises, He will not fail you. It is never God's will for a man to forsake his family. To willfully forsake them is described as being "worse than an infidel." The government may be able to give food stamps, but they can never give the love and care of a live-in father.

Question:

I agree with you that the government should not make moral decisions that the church and church families should make for themselves. But what about the protection of all those people who do not go to church or do not comprehend spiritual authority making these decisions? Who is is going to protect them if not the government?

Answer:

The role of the government is precisely to protect the helpless. Those without the covering of the Church are indeed helpless. But for the government to make moral and ethical decisions for people is inappropriate. That is the reason society is in the moral confusion we are in today. We have acquiesced our responsibilities in decision-making and have called for government to make these decisions for us. The role of government is to protect our rights to make moral decisions. Obviously, some basic laws apply to all societies—laws against murder, stealing, etc. The government needs to recognize basic human rights and ensure that the laws reflect those concepts. But it is never the role of the government to become the interpreter of spiritual laws.

Question:

I understand that recently a seminar was conducted by the American Bar Association on "Tort Legislation and the Church—The Wave of the 1990's." One subtitle was "Piercing the Corporate Veil" with emphasis on how not only to sue churches but also to extend the suit to pastors and deacons and other church officials. One area that was discussed was individuals being influenced by what they hear at church and then claiming they had been "brainwashed." They were taught the fine points of suing on that premise. How can we as Christians respond to this attack on the church?

Answer:

Instruction on such legal strategy is indeed motivated by a satanic attack on the Church. People are "brainwashed" every day. What do you think is the goal of advertising? What do talk shows do but introduce ideas—or more aptly, "brainwash" viewers. We are all creatures with brains. When we send our kids to school, we are saying to the teachers, "Take my child and wash ignorance out of his mind. Replace ignorance with truth and information." Yet, the ABA wishes to accuse religious instructors of "brainwashing!"

The bottom line is that lawyers have sensitized our society into suing people for anything and everything. Who do you think profits from litigations? I think you will find many "suit-happy" lawyers at these seminars are wealthy and influential members of the ABA. What can we do about it? I say we scream bloody murder! Unscrupulous lawyers thrive on intimidation. And as long as we lie down and take it, they will continue to persecute and prosecute us.

Here at Chapel Hill, we have gone to court in order to set legal precedents. They must realize that we will stand up and protect our rights and freedoms on their own battlegrounds—the courts. But we must be cautious and not reckless, giving a place for the devil to attack us. Discretion is still the better part of valor!

Question:

Many people recommend that the United States base its laws on the Bible and the Ten Commandments. Because this foundation for legislation reflects the Judeo-Christian perspective, how would the rights and freedoms of Moslems, Buddhists, even atheists and other people be protected?

Answer:

Most religions adhere to certain basic principles —the respect for and preservation of life and property, protection of children, punishment of criminals, etc. Most recognized religions in the world have similarities in basic codes of ethics. Government should reflect a very broad and basic concept of morality. In my opinion, it is advisable for the government to be broad rather than narrow in its application. If the government chose the Judeo-Christian ethic to base its laws upon, it would inherently protect the rights of all citizens. Scripture bears out that though we may not agree with someone, that does not keep them from being our neighbor and our having certain responsibilities toward them, especially allowing and protecting their rights and freedoms.

Question:

Can you explain the difference between nationalism and ethnic culture? For example, what is the difference in accepting the Scottish Highlanders or some other ethnic group and their celebrations and the African American in their rituals? Is this a form of insidious racism?

Answer:

I think we should all be proud of our heritage and ethnic culture. I can understand the desire of any race or nationality to preserve their traditions as long as traditions are not abusive or demanding. Racism does take many faces, and none of us are exempt from displaying some degree of prejudice. In our effort to protect and perpetuate our social patterns, it is possible for us to become offensive, even racist, in promoting our particular traditions. I readily agree that there have been tremendous inequities among the races in this country. Far too little recognition has been given blacks for their participation and contributions to our history and the development of our country. Nationalities and races aside, our first identity should be our Christian heritage. God is no respecter of persons. Racial and national pride is not evil, but we must recognize first that we are children of God, joint-heirs with Christ Jesus, and partakers of His covenant. We are citizens of the Kingdom of God first.

Question:

Some efforts are being made to pass laws that would hold parents responsible for the criminal actions of their minor children. These laws would lead to evicting families from public housing if their children are involved with selling or use of drugs. I agree that parents do have responsibilities for their children's actions, but it is impossible to monitor kids 24 hours a day. To what degree should parents be held legally responsible for the actions of their children?

Answer:

Perhaps middle class families don't fully realize the scope of this problem because of our environment, and the fact that most of us keep fairly close tabs on our children. But there are many parents today who totally abdicate their responsibilities and have no control over their children. As a result, these children become involved in all types of crimes at an early age. Children as young as 10, 12 years old, some even younger, commit serious crimes. It seems cruel to force parents to pay for the crimes of their children, but the parent is legally, morally, ethically, and spiritually responsible until a child is old enough to make his or her own decisions. I am sure in some cases the parent loses control and thinks he is not responsible for his child's problems. But somewhere that parent has failed—perhaps by allowing them to keep the wrong company, or not requiring them to respect authority, or allowing them to make the decision not to go to church. Some decisions may seem harmless but they can create serious problems later in a child's sense of right and wrong. We cannot abdicate the legal, moral or spiritual responsibilities for our children. Legally, we are responsible until the law says that our children are legal adults. The spiritual responsibilities of parents never ends.

Question:

There are several cases where the families of comatose patients are petitioning for the right to allow their family member to die naturally. Also, there are several cases, one here in Georgia specifically, in which one has been given the right to allow life support systems to be withdrawn. What are your feelings about this issue?

Answer:

Again, such situations with terminally ill family members bring us back to the issue of government controls and intrusion into our own affairs. Allow me to answer the question two ways. First, if I were not a Christian and had no eternal hope, and I lived in constant pain with no hope of relief and I wanted to die, I don't think the government has the right to tell me I can't end my own pain and suffering. That is my decision to make, right or wrong. The government should have no right to tell me what to do. If a family member is comatose, it is the right of the family to make that life or death decision concerning life support, not the government.

However, as a Christian, I would make my decision by totally different guidelines. First of all, life is precious and is a gift of God. God gives and takes away when He sees fit. I trust God for His will to be done in my life. I would pray for God's healing power to bring relief from suffering. However, I do not think a natural death violates Scripture by refusing life support systems that keep a body alive in a vegetable state. By that method we may be doing exactly what some accuse us of doing—playing God. If God wants to take someone, what right do we have to sustain that life against natural causes that would bring an end to life? I fully believe in a committed life. We commit our lives to God and trust Him to sustain us in a productive life. When that has been completed and our course has been finished, there should be dignity in death.

EIGHT

Did We Really Come From Apes?

How do we reconcile scientific fact and religious traditions in the minds of our young students? Do we look like fools in the eyes of scientists? Are there scriptural explanations for creation? Is the earth older than 6,000 years? Where did Cain get his wife? Why is Satan allowed to inhabit this planet?

These are some of the many questions that linger in the minds of our bright young students who want to know truth. God is truth. It is our responsibility to find truth and tell them the real truth . . .

Question:

How do dinosaurs and skeletal remains of early man ("Lucy," Homohabilis and erectus, Neanderthal, and Cro-Magnon) fit in with the biblical account of creation?

Answer:

Dinosaurs and early man do not conflict with the biblical account of creation. The Bible states that the earth was without form and void when God created the Garden of Eden. You must have something already present to "void" it, indicating that something was present on earth before the Garden of Eden. Dinosaurs and early man could easily accommodate this concept without violating scriptural principles. The Bible is a book showing the nature, character and Lordship of Jesus Christ. It is not intended to be a book of science, though it does not contradict nor negate historical integrity. For the Bible to attempt to explain the pre-Garden world to us is beyond its scope and intention. The Bible indicates that the earth along with God's creation is inhabited by evil forces due to the fall of Lucifer and his confinement to this world. This understanding allows for man's capacity to aberrate and counterfeit God's creation and original intent. It is altogether possible that dinosaur-like creatures could be aberrations of Satan. They certainly exhibited great violence. Because of the theory of evolution there is usually an assumption that man developed from a primitive to a more complex state through the years (Ape to modern man). An alternative explanation might be that men placed here before Adam and Eve were corrupted into the forms we find in fossil records by the evil forces which were bound in the earth through Lucifer's fall. The biblical account of Nebuchadnezzar seems to support this.

Question:

Can the concept of evolution ever mesh with biblical accounts of creation? Could Adam and Eve be products of evolution?

Answer:

The answer to both questions is yes, it is possible. If this is the way God chose to accomplish His work, that would certainly be His prerogative. The Bible often uses symbols to explain complex concepts in order that we can more easily understand. It is not God's intention in the Bible to give us a detailed account of His engineering marvels! The difference between Adam and Eve and "early man" is that God breathed His spirit into Adam. This spiritual identity is something "early man" did not have. In my opinion, whether we were created out of thin air, dust or slow changes through time is unimportant to the reason God created mankind. Should evolution be a valid explanation supported by scientific data and fact, God still created the world as a part of His plan. It is important for young minds to understand that God and science rightly understood are not necessarily in conflict. In fact, science can be one of God's greatest tools in bringing comprehension to His marvelous creation. When we totally discount scientific evidence with unsubstantiated theories, we render the cause of God incredible in the minds of bright young people. We must teach them how to reconcile the creation story with God's ultimate intentions.

Question:
Why is animal and plant crossbreeding possible if all animals and plants were created "after their own kind"?

Answer:
Animals and plants cannot crossbreed with anything above their own genus. Only closely related species have the capability of mixing genes that will survive a pregnancy.

Question:
The Bible indicates creation occurred in a six day period. Explain God's concept of a day.

Answer:
I doubt our 24-hour period of a day is the same perspective of time as God's. In fact, the Bible speaks of a day being "as a thousand years" to God. The dimension of time is given to man as a boundary. It is possible that time does not exist in the heavenly realms as we know it in our existence here. Physics has proven, particularly in relativity, that the way you look at things is a matter of perspective—including time. In our world, as you look at things on an atomic scale of atoms and molecules, these particles don't seem to obey the ideas of time as we experience it. At a much greater level, as any object approaches the speed of light, time slows down and eventually stops at light speed. Time is a relative concept. A day was created by God for our measurement of a time frame, not to restrict God.

Question:
If God created the earth for His pleasure

and beauty, why did He allow Satan to inhabit it?

Answer:

God knew Lucifer would rebel against Him. However, we must realize that foreknowledge is not predestination. God also knew that man would disobey and fall from the grace of God. He also knew the only way to "redeem" man was to give him the option of having free moral choice. In order to have this possibility of choice, evil forces must exist. The entire creation of God on the earth, man and planet, has become a battleground between the forces of evil and righteousness. God can only receive glory when man exerts his will to choose the righteousness of God. Had Satan been banished from earth, there would have been no options for man's power to use choice. He would have had only one choice.

Question:

When Cain was driven away from the presence of God because of his crime of murder, where did he find a wife?

Answer:

Like Adam, Cain had been birthed by the "breath" or spirit of God. The Bible doesn't tell us where he got his wife. However, we can speculate based on scientific data coupled with the overall intent of God in creation. It is possible she was a part of a people who existed in the Garden. We only know that God chose to focus on the story of Adam and Eve. Perhaps she was part of a people who existed as a part of the "void" described in Genesis. These people could well be the end product of the development of "early man." This speculation does not violate the intent of biblical accounts of the Garden of Eden and creation.

Question:
Fundamental Christian tradition holds that the earth is 6,000 years old (as counted generationally by Archbishop James Ussher in the 1700s). How is it possible to reconcile this with geographical evidence that shows the earth is 4.5 billion years old, as proven by fossil records and radiometric dating of rocks?

Answer:
There is no conflict between geological evidence (fossils, rock dating) and biblical evidence of the age of earth. Christian tradition is probably in error on this point. Did not Jesus say that we often teach the traditions of men as truth? If you look at a day not as a 24-hour period, but as a symbolic span of time, which God apparently did, it puts a new perspective on the age of the earth.

Question:
What is the explanation for the primitive skeletal remains that seem to link primates to man?

Answer:
First of all, the scientific community admits there are still many gaps to be filled. But presuming this possibility doesn't negate the fact that God could have used primates as a tool of His creation procedure. At what stage of man's development God chose to breathe into him His spirit is open for interpreta-

tion. Focus on two important considerations:

1. God was responsible for the creation and development of man. Period. How He effected it is really immaterial for a spiritual relationship with God, and He purposely did not give any of us enough information to claim to have all the truth.

2. Don't confuse the minds of young people who may write off creation by God as a theory of religious fanatics who don't live in a real world of facts by denying obvious scientific data.

Question:

If all people descended from Adam and Eve, why is there so much variation among them? Doesn't human variety support evolution?

Answer:

People are genetically complex. Even without *considering* evolution, there are enough different combinations of the 46 chromosomes in a person's body to give unique individuality at every birth. Theoretically, evolution is a slow process. It is based on the fact that spontaneous mutations in an individual might give it advantages over others it lives with. Thus, it might be able to survive better and reproduce the mutation. This concept does not violate or contradict my Christian beliefs. I am awed by God's techniques of nature.

Question:

Was the Garden of Eden a real or symbolic place? Where is this "Garden," and what evidence is there for the "Flood"?

Answer:

Whatever you choose to believe—the Garden of Eden as a literal or symbolic place—is unimportant to the fact that it did exist. It very well could have been symbolic, for God repeatedly uses symbols for communication and human comprehension. On the other hand, there are several places lush enough for the Garden to have literally existed—the delta of the Tigris and Euphrates Rivers is often regarded to be a prime spot. But through the centuries, the surface of the earth and even the continents have shifted. The Garden could have been almost anywhere. At one time even Antarctica was a warm, lush, tropical place. There is hard evidence to support this.

As for the flood, little hard archaeological evidence exists to support or refute its occurrence. However, there are scars on the surface of the earth that geologists think were caused by massive erosion from flooding. Usually, scientists think of erosion of the earth's surface as an extremely slow process, taking millions of years. The Appalachian Mountains are approximately 400 million years old if we date the rocks. Yet at their formation, they are assumed to have looked like the Rockies of today, though erosion has been attacking them ever since. But there are exceptions to these slow processes in nature. In the United States, the channeled scablands of Montana, Wyoming and Washington, with deep gorges, cut banks and wide erosion channels, are thought to have been formed in two weeks after a glacial dam melted on an ancient lake to the East. The story of the flood tells an important spiritual saga of man's demise through sin and the destruction of the earth because of the curse of sin. It sets the stage for God's redemption of man and the earth.

Question:

There are some Christians who have an "escape" mentality toward the earth. How does this relate to God's command that we take dominion over the earth and be good stewards of His creation?

Answer:

God loves the earth that He created. He has not given up on it! He does not love the systems of the world that reflect the depravity and sin of men and the reign of Satan on earth with materialism, violence and atheism. We, as Christians, are here to stay. One of the primary purposes of the creation of man was to take dominance over the earth and to bring order to a place filled with disarray. The Garden of Eden was a microcosm of what God intended life to be like.

Question:

Could a lack of responsible stewardship by man over his environment affect the return of Jesus Christ?

Answer:

Jesus exhibited control over natural things—the contrary winds He stilled, the fig tree He cursed, the untamed colt He rode. We must come to this same place of authority over God's creation. Only then will solutions come for the problems man has created: our own garbage, depleted ozone, the greenhouse effect, endangered and extinct animals and plants, etc. Satan has used our irresponsibility to destroy mankind and his habitation. Jesus Christ is looking not only for the redemption of mankind, but also for the redemption of His earth that was cursed by sin. Even as Christ desires a mature Church, His Bride, He desires a reclaimed earth as well. If we seek the face of God, turn from our wicked ways, God will forgive our sin and heal our land.

Question:
Rightly understood, Science is the search for truth. A true scientist will accept truth regardless of its source. Jesus is the Author of truth. Why then do so many Christians deny obvious scientific evidence? Are they not hypocrites within their own religion?

Answer:
True science will never conflict with the Bible. Truth is truth. Truth is not a spiritual concept alone. It is merely the statement of a fact which exists. However, man also needs "absolutes" he can depend upon. Such an absolute is God, and God is indeed Truth. God exemplifies all that is true in every area and time frame. Through erroneous doctrine Satan has convinced many that a chasm exists between science and Christianity. Satan is the author of this "adversary" relationship between the two. Much scientific thought today in many disciplines supports biblical accounts of creation and the development of the earth. The Christian does have the great challenge and responsibility of presenting a coherent premise of how things are to the world. The Bible says that the preaching of the cross is foolish to people who perish. The concept of vicarious suffering and death is difficult for unspiritual people to accept. To the contrary, our lack of understanding natural

developments will never lead men to salvation. In fact, it probably precludes many who otherwise would be receptive to the Gospel.

NINE

Can Sex Be Any Better?

W hat about oral sex . . . is it wrong? Is masturbation a sin? Is AIDS a curse of God on the homosexual? Where does admiration end and lust begin? Is a vasectomy a legitimate option for the Christian husband? What about artificial insemination and test tube babies? Can a homosexual be a Christian?

Sex is on most people's minds. There are many questions they want to ask, but they want the right answer. Here are some answers to some of the questions you always wanted to know the answer to but were afraid to ask . . .

Question:

If marriage and heterosexuality is the biblical standard, why are there so many people today in the gay community?

Answer:

Marriage is the plan of God for the foundation of the family. God made man, male and female. God created man and woman to need one another. Heterosexuality is the biblical standard for relationships in order that the family may recreate itself. Sexuality becomes a bond between a man and a woman. There are many reasons people turn to homosexuality. Many become homosexual because such bonding provides acceptance in intimacy when they have been hurt or spurned in a "normal" relationship. Perhaps we are more aware of people in the "gay" lifestyle because society has encouraged them to "come out of the closet" and declare their sexual preferences. In the past, homosexuality was considered "taboo." Now there is more acceptance of alternative lifestyles in society. But the biblical plan is man and woman entering into a heterosexual relationship, with their sexuality forming a bond between both them for companionship and for reproduction.

Question:

Can one remain in the homosexual lifestyle and still be a Christian?

Answer:

A Christian is that person who has made a public confession that he accepts Jesus Christ as Lord and Savior of his life and has said in his heart that God has raised Christ from the dead (Romans 10:9).

None of us are perfect, for the Bible says we have all sinned and come short of the glory of God. But the Christian has the right of confession and of receiving forgiveness for his sins. However, if one continues to live willfully in a state of sin and rebellion, then reprobation becomes a possibility. This we might call "presumptuous" sin. One may come to know Christ, accept Him as Lord and Savior, but then must deal with his ongoing sins in a state of contrition and strive to deal with every sin in his life that would hinder or destroy his Christian witness.

Question:

Is AIDS a curse of God upon the gay community?

Answer:

All disease and suffering in mankind is a result of sin. If we smoke, we run the high risk of cancer. If we overeat and become obese, we run the risk of heart failure. Statistically, a high incidence of AIDS occurs in the gay community due to their particular lifestyle. However, AIDS is beginning to move into the heterosexual community. If AIDS were a curse just upon homosexuals, it would remain there. Increasingly, anyone who participates in certain sexual activities or in the drug culture risks becoming victim of this disease. I do not believe that God has singled out the homosexual with the curse of AIDS. There are certain physical laws that cannot be broken safely. If they are broken, the transgressor, homosexual or heterosexual, can face serious consequences.

Question:

Is oral sex between consenting married

adults a sin?

Answer:

Oral sex is not specifically dealt with in the Bible. However, there are some principles we should observe that can give us direction. Sex is God's idea and its purpose is not only for procreation, but also for recreation and the development of deep relationship between man and woman. I see nothing wrong with any sexual procedure that does not physically harm or emotionally demean either of the partners. Allow me to add that any sexual technique must be entered into with wholehearted mutual agreement that it adds to the fulfillment and stability of the relationship. On that basis, there is no scriptural proof that oral sex is sinful.

Question:

A court in Florida acquitted a man charged with rape because they said the victim had dressed immodestly and had been at least partially responsible for the attack upon her. What are your views on this decision?

Answer:

A woman does have the responsibility to dress in a way so that she does not make herself vulnerable to attacks by violent men who may misread her intentions. Dressing inappropriately may put her in a vulnerable position but it in no way justifies the actions of the man who may attack and rape her. Rape is still a serious crime of violence and he should bear the consequences of his actions as much as if he attacked any woman dressed in any fashion. A Christian woman bears the responsibility to dress modestly in order not only to protect herself from these violent attacks, but as a witness of her Christian life. Circumstance dictates the proper attire. Swimming calls for swim wear, but even then, discretion should be used. There are modest swimsuits and there are some that leave nothing to the imagination! A woman who wears suggestive clothing is often exhibiting her insecurities and lack of judgment. And even though it is illegal, she could well be setting herself up to be a victim. Discretion is the key for the safety of a woman. Once the damage is done it can't be undone by placing legal responsibility on a rapist. A woman must be more concerned for her safety than who is legally responsible for a violent act against her.

Question:

What is the solution to the need of physical intimacy in a single person's life without compromising virginity or personal morals?

Answer:

Because a person is not married, does not mean that he or she does not have sexual needs and drives. Dealing with these desires properly is important. Sexual drives can be translated into "energy." Many times single people become involved in a ministry to the handicapped, to the infirmed, or to children or in other areas of ministry that utilize their "pent-up" energy. You say this isn't realistic. Webster's defines "sublimate" as "to express socially unacceptable impulses or biological drives in constructive, socially acceptable forms, often unconsciously." Often "self-manipulation" or masturbation becomes a form of release and relief for single persons. The important issue here is what scenes play on the "screen of the mind" and where might that fantasy ultimately lead. However, one should not develop a great sense of guilt for dealing with natural appetites.

Question:

Is it a sin for married partners to engage in mutual masturbation and oral sex?

Answer:

Certain circumstances sometimes require a couple to be innovative in love-making. For example, if the wife is pregnant or has some other physical reason she cannot engage in sexual intercourse, yet has a great desire to be intimate with her husband, the couple might consider alternatives. Or if the husband has some physical limitation that precludes his ability for sexual intercourse, they will need other ways to express intimacy. However, any sexual act should be with the mutual consent of both partners with a mutual enjoyment with neither of them feeling forced or demeaned by the activity. The key is mutual consent and pleasure. But scripturally, it cannot be proven that it is wrong.

Question:

Why are some men able to control their sexual urges while others are unable?

Answer:

Discipline is a Christian virtue, and it does not come easily. Out-of-control sexual urges lead to hurtful relations, unwanted pregnancies and situations that are difficult to resolve. Some men are only concerned with satisfying their sexual needs without concern for consequences. The inability to control any desire including sexual drives, often relates directly to a lack of training in children who are unable to control their emotions. Allowing a child to have a "temper tantrum" without being checked can lead to inability to control other emotions later including sexual drives. Self-control begins early and must be taught.

Question:

I am a Christian married man. Today I drove by a house where a beautiful woman dressed in a two-piece swim suit washing her car caught my eye. I found myself driving by the house four more times looking at her. Now I feel guilty about it and wonder whether I committed adultery in my heart. How do you know when you have gone too far in admiring a pretty woman?

Answer:

Admiring a pretty woman is not sinful in itself. One of the most, if not the most beautiful, graceful, poetic creations of God is a lovely woman. But admiration ceases and lust begins when you say in your heart and mind that you would violate the laws of God and man to have her sexually. If she or you are married, or if you should meet her and you forced yourself upon her in any way, then you violate God's intents and purposes. It is natural for a man to be tempted with certain thoughts when he sees a pretty woman. But to dwell on, encourage, and then enter into fantasy with those thoughts often leads to a mental obsession and eventually steps to see that those fantasies are realized.

Question:

There are archaic laws still on the books in the state of Georgia forbidding oral sex and sodomy even between consenting married adults. Is there scriptural proof that these sexual practices are sinful?

Answer:

No, in my interpretation of Scripture I do not see a scriptural basis for these laws. Many laws on our books are archaic, and some even become an intrusion by the government on the decisions of our private lives. However, some laws have other bases. Sodomy, for example, is usually associated with homosexuality, violent crimes against children, etc. Many of our laws reflect Victorian standards of morality and should be reviewed. Laws governing the consenting actions of a married couple were wrong then and they are wrong now. If some of these practices between consenting adults are ruled illegal, I contend those laws constitute an intrusion upon personal privacy by the government. The church should have the right to establish moral guidelines to build solid family and social relationships. One other consideration should be personal health. If a couple wishes to engage in "exotic" sexual practices, perhaps they should consult a medical doctor to find out what health risks they may be taking in transmission of diseases, infections, etc.

Question:

Are there any reasons from a scriptural standpoint that prohibits sexual intercourse during a woman's menstrual period? I heard a minister say that God forbade it in the Old Testament, and He must have had a good reason. Some women have extended periods, and if a husband waits until it is over, the wait is long and difficult. There may be medical reasons for abstinence that I am not aware of, but aside from those, is it a sin?

Answer:

We must understand the reasons God gave certain laws in the Old Testament. Circumstances were quite different then than the way we live today. For example, God forbade people from eating certain types of food in the Old Testament. Today we have learned that when those foods are ill prepared, serious medical problems result. Obviously they did not have the modern equipment we have today—no refrigeration, high cooking heat, and preservatives in food preparation. God knew that the people would not understand the dangers, so He simply said not to eat that type of food. Sanitary conditions were not good then. For that reason, God said certain sexual practices were inappropriate under certain conditions. The New Testament, however, came not to destroy the law but to fulfill it, and to help us understand God's laws more completely. A first consideration of sexual intercourse during the menstrual period of a woman is her comfort. Menstruation can be painful for her. To add to her discomfort is thoughtless. If, however, there is no pain or discomfort for either partner, and there is a mutual desire, my interpretation of that law, according to New Testament understanding, is that Scripture does not forbid it.

Question:

I am a single adult who lives alone. I desire companionship, but for whatever reasons, perhaps my timidity, I have a very lonely social life. I am a normal, healthy adult with sexual desires and drives. I want to deal with them in the right way. Until God provides a mate for me, what sexual outlets are appropriate for me as a Christian? Is masturbation an option?

Answer:

Masturbation itself is neither right nor wrong. It is a physical act. However, it is difficult to achieve a physical release without the participation of the mind. What is on the "screen of the mind" becomes very important. One problem that often occurs in these situations is that a person becomes "addicted" to self-gratification as a lifestyle and never seeks to establish a normal relationship with a woman. It is often easier to retreat into a solitary world where we are not threatened by the intimacy of someone else than to run the risk of rejection or failure. We will never know whether we can succeed in forming relationships until we move toward developing them. A good way to overcome timidity is to force yourself to move out of your solitary lifestyle by making friends. Good friendships can lead to a deeper relationship and, ultimately, marriage.

Question:

My husband and I have been married 6 years and have 4 children. In order to limit our family size, my husband is considering having a vasectomy. Some people consider any form of birth control a sin. I recall the story in the

Bible of God striking a man dead for spilling his semen on the ground. We want to do the right thing. What do you suggest?

Answer:

When considering a vasectomy, the purpose for this medical solution is important. If it is for the purpose of freedom for promiscuousness, then it is wrong. If it is for the control of the size of the family, then a vasectomy is no different than any other type of birth control. If you have decided that you don't want to have more children, then in my opinion, a vasectomy is an alternative. However, this procedure should be done with the full consent of the wife and with professional medical advice. You should realize that in many cases a vasectomy is irrevocable. Medical technology is trying to perfect methods to reverse the procedure. A young man in his twenties should give careful consideration before doing it. You never know what will happen to your family. What if a car accident wiped out a man's wife and all their children? Would he ever want to have more children? These are questions that should be considered before making this very important decision.

Question:

Are artificial insemination and test tube babies unscriptural or sinful?

Answer:

The word "artificial" gives insight into the ethics of the problem. These procedures circumvent human involvement and the bonds that are created through sexual relationships between a man and a woman. Such scientific advances also could lead to controlling the population of the earth and dictating by law yet another personal and private right of the individual. Laws will be enacted to control births increasingly. The government could feasibly say who can and who cannot have babies, etc. However, if these procedures serve to aid childless couples seeking the help of medical technology to conceive a baby, the motive is very different. We have seen litigation recently in similar situations in which frozen embryos are contested in court by a couple going through divorce proceedings. This is not pleasing to God. My feeling is that as long as families can be created naturally, this is God's plan. Anything that thwarts or circumvents the plan of God is wrong.

TEN

Conclusion

The questions that have been asked in this book just scratch the surface of the many questions that life presents us. We have tried to answer these hard questions out of years of experience in ministry and based upon principles of the Word of God.

We fully realize that many people who are not Christians will read this book. We would like for them to begin to see that Christianity is more than a theological creed—it is a way of life that provides answers and solutions to the sticky and troublesome questions of life.

There are many other questions that confront us

daily which were not addressed in this book. In later books we will answer those questions for we are convinced that Jesus Christ has answers and solutions for all questions we face.

Obviously, the answers we have given here reflect our theological convictions. However, they are based upon sound and orthodox principles of God's Word. This book was not designed to be a scriptural textbook, but rather statements and guidelines for living based upon principles of the Bible as we interpret them through the guidance of the Holy Spirit.

We would like to express our appreciation to some who have worked to make this book effective and relevant.

Pat Harwell is a psychologist. A devout Christian, Pat bases her professional career not only upon her academic background, but upon years of experience as a practicing family counselor. She has provided valuable insight and input to the answers in this book.

Scott Huckaby is a bright young scientist who has assisted on this book, providing scientific data and perspective that proves God is indeed the framer of all things and the Master of the universe. His scholarly approach to science based upon his own Christian convictions provides him the ability to prove to young minds the existence and purposes of God in all of nature and creation.

Tricia Weeks, an educator and writer, has added her valuable input to the writing of this book. Having served not only as an educator and as a writer but as a public relations liaison at Chapel Hill, she understands the need to present a book that is credible.

We also wish to express appreciation to staff members and volunteers who participated in this endeavor. Donna Eubanks, Angie Martin, Dawn Brewer, Pat Mortensen, Annette Eubanks, Rob Stanborough, Janice McFarland and LaDonna Paulk provided technical skills in proofreading, transcribing, typesetting, photography, and in the graphic arts. Also a special thanks to Wes Bonner of Kingdom Publishers for coordinating the project.

Finally, I would like to thank Bishop Earl Paulk for his ability to provide us these answers in a pragmatic yet spiritual manner. His forty-five years of practical ministry—counseling, comforting, advising—have prepared him to be a credible resource for answers and solutions in our society today. He has given himself totally to the work of the Kingdom of God, showing the world that Jesus Christ is The Answer.

—DON PAULK

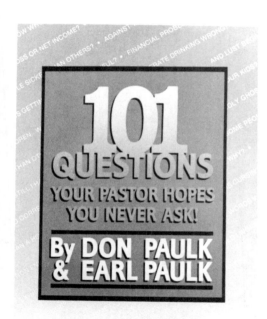

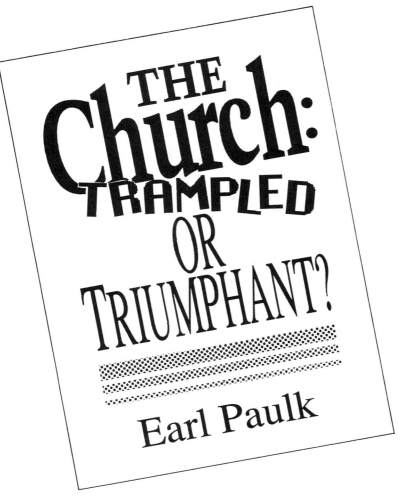

Is the modern Church trampled beyond repair, or is the
Church triumphant in offering society solutions and
direction for the 21st Century? Earl Paulk insists that the
Church has not become as salt without flavor, good for
nothing but to be trampled under the foot of public
opinion and media ridicule. Instead, Earl Paulk issues a
proclamation of hope. The fire of this proclamation will
ignite Christians who sit passively behind sanctuary walls.
And for people searching for solutions, it's a proclamation
worth considering.

Order form, see page 143

Finally! The authoritative Q and A Book on the Kingdom of God is here!

NOW YOU CAN FIND OUT WHAT THE GOSPEL OF THE KINGDOM MEANS TO YOU–

–because Earl Paulk has responded with straightforward, biblical answers to twenty of the most frequently asked questions on the Kingdom of God.

20/20 VISION is the "Everything you always wanted to know" book on the hottest topic to hit Christianity in your lifetime.

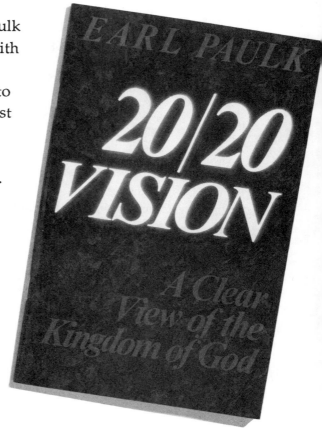

Order form, see page 143

THIS BEST-SELLER IS RATED "R"...

... for "real." It's real because it's frank, funny and sensitive.

And because it takes sex out of the bedroom and dares to mix it with the rest of life. If you've been looking for a primer on healthy relationships to share with your whole family, or if you're ready to take the next step in intimacy with your beloved, *Sex Is God's Idea* is a great idea for you.

Order form, see page 143

Anyone can see symptoms. But it takes the eye of a physician to see the infirmity... and the skill of a surgeon to cut it away.

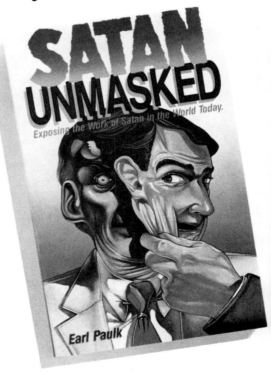

In this penetrating look at the patterns of evil, Earl Paulk exposes the blatant attacks against you and your family. And he delves beneath the surface to confront even the subtlest strategies meant to keep you from changing the world you live in.

Order form, see page 143

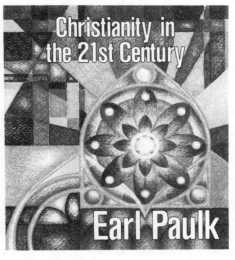

YOU'VE NEVER READ A BOOK LIKE THIS ONE.

Spiriual Megatrends not only prepares you for the changes you and your family will encounter as our world shifts gears for the twenty-first century, it gives you a rare cutaway glimpse of the spiritual moves which underlie every transition you'll face in the coming decade. With sharp insight into the years ahead and a firm grip on life today, Earl Paulk gives you, in Spiritual Megatrends, a glimpse of the future when you need it most–right now.

Order form, see page 143

Go Ahead.
Laugh.
Out Loud.

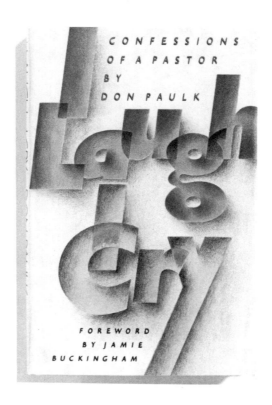

Or turn the page and test your tenderness with an old-fashioned tearjerker. So what if someone sees you. There's nothing like a good book to make you appreciate life. And there's nothing like the collection of recollections and stories in Don Paulk's *I Laugh, I Cry* to make you glad you're alive–even after a day like today.

Order form, see page 143

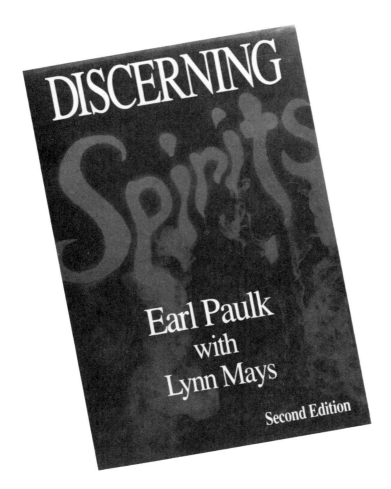

Spirits. The unseen forces that can drive your mind, provoke your emotions and force your life out of the bounds of control.

In this four-tape package, Earl Paulk and Lynn Mays examine the spiritual roots of:

- emotional outbursts
- uncontrollable spending
- mental torment

- abuse
- addiction
- crippling insecurity

If you find yourself locked into habits and attitudes that keep you struggling, this series could be the key to your freedom.

Order form, see page 143

Kingdom Publishers

P.O. Box 7300 • Atlanta, GA 30357

Name _____

Address _____

City _____ State _____ Zip _____

Telephone (____) _____

QTY.	TITLE		PRICE	AMT.
	101 Questions Your Pastor Hopes You Never Ask *hardcover*	*Don Paulk & Earl Paulk*	$12.95	
	The Church: Trampled or Triumphant?	*Earl Paulk*	9.95	
	20/20 Vision	*Earl Paulk*	2.50	
	Sex Is God's Idea	*Earl Paulk*	7.95	
	Satan Unmasked	*Earl Paulk*	9.95	
	Spiritual Megatrends	*Earl Paulk*	8.95	
	I Laugh, I Cry *hardcover*	*Don Paulk*	12.95	
	Discerning Spirits *(4-tape series)*	*Earl Paulk & Lynn Mays*	20.00	
			Total	
			Postage & Handling	$2.00
			TOTAL DUE	

Enclose check or money order for full amount
and mail along with this order form to:

Post Office Box 7300
Atlanta, Georgia 30357